ALL SORTS OF TAPAS

To my husband Reg.
You patiently listened to all my suggestions, tasted ALL my attempts
and still managed to show enthusiasm once it was all done. Thank you.
PS: Mom, this book wouldn't have been the same without you!

CHANTAL LASCARIS

Published in 2021 by Struik Lifestyle
an imprint of Penguin Random House South Africa (Pty) Ltd
Company Reg. No. 1953/000441/07
The Estuaries, 4 Oxbow Crescent, Century Avenue, Century City, 7441
PO Box 1144, Cape Town 8000, South Africa
www.penguinrandomhouse.co.za

Publisher: Beverley Dodd
Managing editor: Cecilia Barfield
Designer: Helen Henn
Editor: Linda de Villiers
Proofreader: Thea Grobbelaar
Indexer: Cecilia Barfield
Photographer: Donna Lewis
Photographer's assistant: Malizo Masumpa
Stylist: Caro Alberts
Stylist's assistant: Lize Buitendag

Reproduction by Studio Repro and Hirt & Carter Cape (Pty) Ltd
Printed and bound in China by Toppan Leefung
Packaging and Printing (Dongguan) Co., Ltd.

MENGSEL
Papier van
verantwoordelike bronne
FSC® C104723
www.fsc.org

CONTENTS

INTRODUCTION

Welcome to the wonderful world of tapas – those small tasty dishes that you can eat all day long. Served in bars all over Spain, good tapas are all about the perfect marriage of food, drink and sparkling conversation. It's the ideal combination of little dishes packed with big flavours.

Anyone who knows me knows that I love two things (well, let's say two 'main' things) – food and travel. Writing this book has been such a great opportunity for me to bring these two passions together into one recipe compilation.

My inspiration comes from the source – the bustling nightlife of the Spanish tapas bars and, my favourite, the pintxos bars of San Sebastian (the food capital of the world). I've been lucky enough to spend some time in Spain and love the enthusiasm that the Spaniards have for the sheer joy of eating and drinking. They approach each dish as if it were a celebration. I love the way that eating tapas is not a solo affair; they are meant to be enjoyed with the people around you. You're not all just focused on your own dish, rather you're passing plates around and constantly connecting and sharing while you eat. Tapas are also the perfect way to satisfy those indecisive taste buds and avoid your food FOMO when you can't quite decide what you want to eat. What I also enjoy about this way of eating is that I don't only have to eat them when I'm entertaining or cooking for others, they're just as good to snack on all by myself.

But where did it all start? I like the popular royal version. Way back in the 13th century King Alfonso X of Castile was recuperating from an illness which meant that he could only eat and drink small portions. He recovered from his illness, and believed his improvement was due to the way he was eating and drinking. He was so happy to be healthy again that, as kings tend to do, he decreed that from henceforth any drink that was served had to be accompanied by a small snack. The truth is probably more along the lines that originally bars had standing room only, so the only place to put your plate was on top of your drink. To reinforce this, the word 'tapa' means 'a cover' or 'a lid'.

Spain is made up of 17 different regions, each priding itself on its own unique gastronomy. To keep it simple, I've concentrated my recipes on tapas and the lesser-known pintxos. Tapas are said to have originated in central Spain, while pintxos are from the north, in Basque Country. Those who live there have a strong identity and culture, even having their own language. Hence the word 'pinchos' is Spanish, while in the Basque language it's spelt 'pintxos'.

Tapas and pintxos are quite different. One tapa or many tapas are essentially small versions of traditional plates of food, whereas pintxos are served with bread as the base, with a selection of toppings all held together with a toothpick.

When you look at different cultures, you'll find that eating smaller plates is not unique to Spain. You'll find antipasti in Italy, mezze in Greece, Morocco, Israel, Turkey and Lebanon, and hors d'eouvres in France. All around the world, you'll find appetisers and snacks in restaurants and bars, on dinner tables and buffets.

In this book, I've included recipes for both tapas and pintxos and have even substituted potato slices for slices of bread, to create my own versions of pintxos. I have tried to bring to life the richness of Spain's regional variations, styles and attitudes while incorporating some uniquely South African flavours. This selection also incorporates as many international-fusion flavours and styles as possible.

This ultimately results in my personal take on Spanish tapas with recipes that are practical yet still exciting.

Each chapter holds recipes that cover a variety of ingredients, from calamari and chorizo to paprika and peppadews, so that you can find a recipe that will suit your taste, or uses ingredients that you happen to have on hand. My hope is that these little paintings will be a feast for the eyes and a feast for the tummy. Using simple, readily available ingredients, you can now whip up a tapas feast that will make you the talk of the town at every get-together. Tapas are truly Spain's gift to the world of great cooking, and I hope this book lets you enjoy the freshest and most fun way to eat with friends and family, all from the comfort of your own kitchen.

I have written this book, as well as all the other books in the *All Sorts of* series, because of my continuing love for cooking healthy food. It never feels like a chore when I'm working away in the kitchen designing meals that are good to look at and even better to eat. I hope my passion comes across in this collection and that my ideas and experiences will allow you to prepare delicious tidbits that will impress your family, friends and, most importantly, yourself.

Salud! Raise a glass to tasty tapas.

(Each recipe contains between 10 and 16 portions, unless stated otherwise.)

Chantal Lascaris

METRIC TO CUP/SPOON CONVERSIONS

Metric	Teaspoons	Metric	Cups
2ml	¼ tsp	60ml	¼ cup
3ml	½ tsp	80ml	⅓ cup
5ml	1 tsp	125ml	½ cup
10ml	2 tsp	160ml	⅔ cup
20ml	4 tsp	200ml	¾ cup
		250ml	1 cup
Metric	Tablespoons	375ml	1½ cups
15ml	1 Tbsp	500ml	2 cups
30ml	2 Tbsp	750ml	3 cups
45ml	3 Tbsp	1 litre	4 cups
60ml	4 Tbsp		

BRUNCH

I absolutely adore a good brunch. While breakfast is usually a rushed and flurried affair, needed to get you going in the morning, brunch is much more laid-back. Breakfast is all about coffee, toast and orange juice, but once those Bloody Marys come out, you know it's brunch time. Brunch isn't so much about eating a meal as it is about having an experience. Leisurely and a little indulgent, brunch is light, sociable and a whole lot of fun.

For me, the very best brunches are tranquil, drawn-out weekend meet-ups, enjoyed with good company, where you can take the time to talk, laugh, reminisce, and of course eat. The timing of brunch means that the menu can offer a wide variety of sweet and savoury options, perfect for those indecisive eaters who just can't make up their minds and would rather have a bit of everything. Best of all, no-one needs to feel guilty by tucking straight into the sweeter flavours of brunch.

Tapas and brunch are a match made in heaven. This selection of brunch offerings runs the gamut from sweet treats such as strawberry French toast bites to superbly savoury items and classic tapas such as the onion and potato tortilla. Eggs are a perennial favourite on brunch tables and there is no shortage of delicious flavour combinations here, from the Caesar-style eggs to eggs *en cocotte*.

A common dilemma with brunch is to decide between savoury or sweet, but here there are some recipes that blend the two. How about savoury avocado toast with pear, Brie, and deliciously sweetened honeyed walnuts?

This selection of stunning brunch tapas allows you to create a luscious spread for the brunch table, where there is something for every taste. Boasting hybrids of your favourite lunch and breakfast items with an unexpected twist or two, this selection can't be beaten. So, the next time you want to host a little get-together for your friends, there's no better way to do that than over some decadent and delightful brunch tapas.

SALAMI, EGG & CHIPS PINTXOS

THESE CRUNCHY LITTLE MORSELS ARE A MAINSTAY IN SPANISH PINTXOS BARS AND EVERYONE HAS THEIR OWN VERSION. I MAKE MINE WITH SALAMI, EGGS AND A LEKKER OVEN-BAKED CHIP OR TWO. APART FROM ITS WONDERFUL TASTE, SALAMI IS A GOOD SOURCE OF NUTRIENTS, VITAMINS AND MINERALS, AND HAS LOADS OF PROTEIN, SO WHILE THIS WILL ONLY TAKE MINUTES TO MAKE, IT WILL LEAVE YOUR GUESTS FEELING FULLER FOR LONGER. THIS SPEEDY BREAKFAST PINTXO IS THE ULTIMATE NO-FUSS PARTY FOOD THAT ALWAYS GETS A WARM RECEPTION.

32 frozen oven chips
16 slices French baguette
butter for spreading
2 Tbsp cooking oil
16 small eggs

16 slices salami
toothpicks (optional)
salt and pepper to taste
chilli flakes (optional)

1. Bake the chips according to the instructions on the packet.
2. Toast the baguette slices and then butter one side.
3. In a pan, heat the oil and fry the eggs until just well done. You might need to fry the eggs in batches.
4. To serve, place a slice of salami on top of each buttered slice of baguette.
5. Add a fried egg, then top with 2 or 3 oven chips and secure with a toothpick, if using.
6. Season with salt and pepper and chilli flakes, if using, and serve immediately.

CHUNKY PHYLLO CIGARS WITH ANCHOVY CREAM CHEESE FILLING

ANCHOVIES ARE QUINTESSENTIALLY SPANISH AND HAVE PLAYED A FUNDAMENTAL ROLE IN THEIR REGIONAL COOKING FOR CENTURIES AND ARE NOW PREPARED AND EATEN ALL OVER THE WORLD. THE SPANISH ENJOY EATING THEM CURED OR FRESH WITH A SIMPLE OLIVE OIL DRESSING. IT'S BELIEVED THE ANCIENT GREEKS BROUGHT THE ART OF SALTING TO THE SPANISH SHORES AND THEY'VE BEEN CURING ANCHOVIES EVER SINCE. CURING THE FISH INTENSIFIES THE FLAVOUR, SO I'VE CREATED A POWERFUL YET CREAMY TASTE SENSATION USING ANCHOVIES CURED AND STORED IN OIL. YOU WILL NEED CANNOLI TUBES TO MAKE THE PHYLLO CIGARS.

MAKES ABOUT 18 CIGARS

1½ sheets phyllo pastry
1 cup cream cheese
2 tsp plain full cream yoghurt
2 Tbsp capers, halved

3 Tbsp mashed anchovies, from a jar
2 tsp fresh dill
extra dill for garnishing (optional)

1. Preheat the oven to 180°C.
2. Slice the phyllo sheets into 4cm x 20cm long lengths, making about 18 pieces.
3. Grease the cannoli tubes and neatly wrap the pieces of phyllo around the tubes. Depending on how long your tube is, you can wrap 3–4 pieces of phyllo per tube.
4. Place the tubes on a greased baking sheet and bake in the oven for a few minutes until golden.
5. Remove from the oven and allow to cool.
6. Once cool enough to handle, carefully remove the phyllo casings from the tubes and set aside.
7. Combine the filling ingredients.
8. To assemble, carefully place about 2 teaspoons of the filling into each phyllo casing. Sprinkle dill onto each end, if using, and serve.

SMOKED SALMON, SCRAMBLED EGG & SAFFRON CUCUMBER BITES

ALTHOUGH SAFFRON ORIGINATED IN ASIA MINOR AND WAS BROUGHT TO SPAIN BY THE MOORS, IT'S STILL CONSIDERED ONE OF THE INTEGRAL INGREDIENTS IN SPANISH COOKING. IT'S ESTIMATED THAT THREE-QUARTERS OF THE WORLD'S PRODUCTION OF THIS VALUABLE FLOWER IS GROWN IN SPAIN. USED HERE, IT'S HELPED CREATE THESE BEAUTIFUL BREAKFAST BITES THAT WILL DEFINITELY PUT A SMILE ON YOUR GUESTS' FACES. IN CASE YOU NEEDED ANOTHER REASON TO INDULGE, THE ADDITION OF SMOKED SALMON HAS ADDED BENEFITS TO YOUR HEALTH. A SINGLE SERVING OF SMOKED SALMON CONTAINS A WHOPPING 136% OF YOUR RECOMMENDED DAILY INTAKE OF VITAMIN B_{12}.

½ medium cucumber
4 large eggs
½ Tbsp butter
salt and pepper to taste
85g smoked salmon ribbons
chives for garnishing

SAFFRON SAUCE
a pinch of saffron
¼ cup warm water
½ cup white wine
50g butter
½ cup cream
a small pinch of salt

1. To make the sauce, soak the saffron threads in the warm water. The water will turn golden yellow from the saffron.
2. Add the white wine to a pan and simmer over a medium heat until reduced to 2 or 3 tablespoons.
3. Stir in the butter and add the cream, a small pinch of salt and the saffron-infused water, including the saffron threads. Simmer over medium heat, stirring until the sauce thickens and turns yellow. Remove from the heat and allow to cool slightly.
4. Slice the cucumber, slightly on the diagonal, into 12–14 slices, about 5mm thick. Refrigerate until ready to serve.
5. Add the eggs to a bowl and whisk until well blended.
6. In a pan, melt the butter and when it begins to bubble, pour in the eggs. Use a wooden spoon to swirl the eggs in small circles around the pan until they look slightly thickened and very small curds begin to form. When the eggs are softly set and slightly runny in places, remove the pan from the heat and leave for a few seconds to finish cooking.
7. Season the eggs with salt and pepper, give one more stir and place a spoonful or two on each cucumber slice.
8. Top each bite with smoked salmon, saffron sauce and a garnishing of chopped chives.

CHIA SEED POWERHOUSE

CHIA SEEDS ARE POWERFUL LITTLE THINGS AND WITH NEARLY 5 GRAMS OF FIBRE PER TABLESPOON AND HIGH LEVELS OF OMEGA-3 FATTY ACIDS, CALLING THIS BREAKFAST A POWERHOUSE IS NO EXAGGERATION. BEST OF ALL YOU CAN ENJOY THIS FOR BREAKFAST, AS A SNACK, OR EVEN AS A HEALTHY DESSERT. IT'S LOADED WITH HEALTH BENEFITS FROM THE PAPAYA, CHIA SEEDS AND GREEK YOGHURT.

1½ cups chia seeds
4 cups milk
2 Tbsp vanilla essence
⅓ cup honey
1½ cups granola, store bought
2 cups Greek yoghurt
3 cups puréed papaya
toasted coconut flakes for garnishing

1. Combine the chia seeds, milk, vanilla essence and honey in a bowl. Mix well and refrigerate overnight so that the chia seeds can thicken.
2. When ready to assemble, give the mixture a good stir to break up any possible lumps.
3. Place about 2 tablespoons of granola in the base of a glass, followed by about 3 tablespoons of chia seed mixture, creating a layer over the granola. Then add about 3 tablespoons of Greek yoghurt on top of the chia seeds and finally add about 4 tablespoons of papaya purée.
4. Sprinkle over some toasted coconut flakes and serve.

Smoked salmon, scrambled egg & saffron cucumber bites

Chia seed powerhouse

FRENCH TOAST BITES WITH STRAWBERRY & HONEY SAUCE

FRENCH TOAST MAY SEEM A BIT INDULGENT BUT IT'S ACTUALLY A GREAT WAY TO ADD IRON AND CALCIUM TO YOUR DIET. THESE BITES ARE ALSO SO MUCH FUN TO EAT THAT YOU'LL MAKE THEM EVEN WHEN NOBODY ELSE IS AROUND. THE STRAWBERRY SAUCE IS SUPER SIMPLE TO MAKE AND TAKES THESE ITSY-BITSY BUNDLES TO NEW HEIGHTS, BEING CREAMY, SOFT, WARM AND CRISP, ALL ROLLED INTO ONE.

3–4 large eggs
1 cup milk
½ tsp salt
1 Tbsp sugar
1 tsp vanilla essence
1 tsp ground cinnamon
4 slices white bread
about 60g butter for frying
crème fraîche to finish

STRAWBERRY HONEY SAUCE
¼ cup honey
2 Tbsp lemon juice
100g fresh strawberries, chopped (keep a few halved strawberries for garnishing)

1. To make the sauce, warm the honey in a small pot over low heat, stirring until thinned but not hot.
2. Remove from the heat and add the lemon juice and strawberries. Stir until blended, cover and let stand at room temperature until ready to serve. (You can blend this with a stick blender once cooled if you prefer a smoother texture.)
3. Whisk together the eggs, milk, salt, sugar, vanilla and cinnamon in a flattish bowl that is wide enough to dip the bread into.
4. Place the bread slices one at a time into the egg mixture and flip to make sure both sides are well coated but not too soaked.
5. Melt the butter in a large pan. Place the bread slices into the pan and cook on medium heat until golden brown on each side, 2–3 minutes.
6. Remove from the heat and cut into bite-size squares.
7. Serve while still warm with a drizzle of strawberry honey sauce and a dollop of crème fraîche. Garnish with the halved fresh strawberries.

POTATO 'TOASTS' WITH EGG, SUMAC & PEA SPREAD

POTATO SLICES ARE THE PERFECT GLUTEN-FREE ALTERNATIVE TO CONVENTIONAL TOASTED BREAD AS THEY'RE STILL STURDY ENOUGH TO HOLD THIS DELICIOUS ASSORTMENT OF TOPPINGS. THE CREAMINESS OF THE PEA AND RICOTTA SPREAD CONTRASTS PERFECTLY WITH THE LEMONY FLAVOUR OF THE ANCIENT MIDDLE EASTERN SPICE, SUMAC. YOU COULDN'T WALK THROUGH THE FOOD MARKETS CENTURIES AGO WITHOUT COMING ACROSS THIS TANGY AND VERSATILE SPICE. LUCKILY FOR US, IT'S READILY AVAILABLE IN MOST SUPERMARKETS.

3 large whole potatoes, unpeeled
2–3 Tbsp oil
½ cup peas, cooked
¾ cup ricotta cheese
2 Tbsp plain full cream yoghurt
salt and pepper to taste

6 slices bacon
20–24 eggs
6 Tbsp milk
sumac for sprinkling
chives for garnishing (optional)

1. Cook the potatoes in boiling water until almost done.
2. Remove the potatoes and, once cool enough to handle, cut them into 1cm-thick slices.
3. In a pan, heat a tablespoon of oil and lightly fry the potatoes on both sides until browned. You might have to do this in batches.
4. In a bowl, roughly mash the peas and combine with the ricotta cheese and yoghurt. Season with salt and pepper.
5. Slice the bacon pieces in half and cook until crisp. Remove and drain on paper towel.
6. Add the eggs and milk to a bowl, season generously with salt and pepper and whisk well until frothy.
7. Pour into a preheated pan and cook, stirring regularly. Once the scrambled eggs are almost cooked, remove the pan from the heat and stir the eggs again.
8. To serve, spread a tablespoon or two of the pea and ricotta mixture onto each potato slice. Place a piece of bacon on top, followed by 1 or 2 tablespoons of scrambled egg. Garnish with a generous sprinkling of sumac, and chives, if using.

EGGS *EN COCOTTE* WITH TOMATO & GOAT'S MILK CHEESE

FEW DISHES ARE QUITE AS EASY TO MAKE AND AS IMPRESSIVE TO PRESENT TO A TABLEFUL OF GUESTS AS THE GLORIOUS EGG *EN COCOTTE. COCOTTE* MEANS 'CASSEROLE' IN FRENCH AND THIS DELICIOUS DISH GETS ITS NAME BECAUSE THE EGGS ARE BAKED IN 'CASSEROLE' DISHES. WHILST THE EGGS ARE NESTLED IN THE CREAMY SAUCE, THE TOPPING GETS AN ADDED TOUCH OF CRISPNESS BY PLACING THE DISHES UNDER THE GRILL. THIS DISH HAS SIMPLE YET TASTY INGREDIENTS, PERFECT FOR THOSE LAZY SUNDAY BRUNCHES.

12 tomatoes, finely chopped
3 onions, finely chopped
¼–½ cup olive oil
¼ cup sugar or sugar substitute
¼ cup chopped fresh basil
¼ cup red wine vinegar

12 slices cooked ham, roughly chopped
½ cup cream
12 eggs
24 slices goat's milk cheese
  (or about 2 logs)
extra fresh basil for garnishing

1. Preheat the oven to 180°C.
2. Grease 12 ramekins.
3. In a pot, gently simmer the tomatoes and onions in the oil until the onion starts to soften.
4. Add the sugar, basil and vinegar and stir together. Simmer until the mixture starts to caramelise.
5. Divide the tomato mixture and then the chopped ham among the 12 ramekins. Add 2 tablespoons of cream to each ramekin.
6. Break an egg into each ramekin, crumble about 2 tablespoons of goat's milk cheese around each egg and bake in the oven for about 15 minutes.
7. Turn the oven to grill and grill for about 5 minutes until the eggs are done to your liking.
8. To serve, season with salt and pepper, garnish with fresh basil and serve warm.

RICOTTA-STUFFED DATES WRAPPED IN BACON

DATES ARE AN INTERESTING FOOD. THEY ARE SWEET AND STICKY WITH CARAMEL TONES AND ARE PERFECTLY PRIMED TO GO WELL WITH SALTY BACON. THEY ARE ALSO INTERESTING WHEN IT COMES TO NUTRITION AS THEY CONTAIN SEVERAL TYPES OF ANTIOXIDANTS THAT HELP PREVENT THE DEVELOPMENT OF ILLNESSES SUCH AS HEART DISEASE AND DIABETES. CREAMY RICOTTA CHEESE STUFFED INTO SWEET DATES AND WRAPPED UP IN SMOKY BACON CREATE A CRISP BUT SOFT BITE OF PERFECTION.

---

12 Medjool dates, pitted
200g streaky bacon (1 packet)
40g ricotta cheese
¼ tsp ground ginger
¼ tsp grated nutmeg
12 toothpicks

1. Preheat the oven to 220°C.
2. If the dates aren't pitted, cut the dates lengthways and remove the pip. If they are pitted, slice them lengthways but don't cut all the way through.
3. Cut the bacon in half lengthwise to make twice as many slices and set aside.
4. In a bowl, combine the ricotta, ginger and nutmeg.
5. Place about a quarter teaspoon of ricotta mixture into each slit date.
6. Wrap a slice of bacon around each ricotta-stuffed date and secure with a toothpick.
7. Arrange all the prepared dates on a greased baking sheet, allowing some space between each one to ensure that they brown evenly.
8. Roast for about 15 minutes, turning halfway through the cooking time, until the bacon is brown and crisp.
9. Remove the sheet from the oven and allow the dates to cool slightly before serving.

AVOCADO TOAST WITH PROSCIUTTO, PEAR & BRIE

THE EXTRAORDINARY AVOCADO HAS BECOME AN INCREDIBLY POPULAR FOOD AMONG HEALTH-CONSCIOUS INDIVIDUALS AS IT IS GREAT FOR BONE AND HEART HEALTH AND IS OFTEN REFERRED TO AS A SUPERFOOD. ITS CREAMY TEXTURE AND SUBTLE FLAVOUR ARE SUPER TOO. COMBINED WITH THE FLAVOURS OF PEAR, BRIE AND PROSCIUTTO, THIS UNASSUMING SOURDOUGH TOAST IS TURNED INTO SOMETHING TRULY SPECIAL. THE ADDITION OF THE HONEYED WALNUTS BRINGS ALL THAT FLAVOUR HOME, QUITE UNAPOLOGETICALLY.

1 avocado, pitted and peeled
1 Tbsp lemon juice
salt and pepper to taste
6–12 slices sourdough bread (depending on size of bread)
1–2 ripe pears, cut into 3mm-thick slices
2 x 125g Brie cheese, cut into 3mm-thick slices
70g prosciutto

12 rocket leaves
olive oil for drizzling
2 tsp honey
2 Tbsp crushed walnuts

1. Mash the avocado, pour over the lemon juice and season with salt and pepper. Mix well.
2. Toast the bread and spread the mashed avocado over the toast.
3. To assemble, lay the pear slices on top of the avocado, followed by some slices of Brie.
4. Tear the prosciutto into pieces and drape over the Brie.
5. Lay the rocket leaves on top and drizzle over a touch of olive oil. Season with salt and pepper.
6. Combine the honey and crushed walnuts and dab some on top of the rocket.

POTATO & ONION TORTILLA

OTHERWISE KNOWN AS *TORTILLAS DE PATATAS,* THIS TRADITIONAL SPANISH OMELETTE HAS BEEN AROUND SINCE THE 1500s. YOU'LL FIND IT ON EVERY TAPAS BAR MENU THROUGHOUT SPAIN, FROM THE MOST BASIC TO THE FANCIEST OF RESTAURANTS. THEY ALL HAVE THEIR OWN VERSION, WHICH IS WHY SOME MIGHT CALL IT SPAIN'S NATIONAL DISH. FOR ME ITS BEAUTY LIES IN ITS SIMPLICITY. WHAT COULD BE BETTER THAN POTATOES AND ONIONS? GOLDEN, YUMMY AND MOIST IN THE CENTRE, THIS IS A BRUNCH-TIME EGG DISH THAT CAN'T BE BEATEN.

¼ cup vegetable oil
2 potatoes, peeled and sliced
2 onions, sliced
1 green pepper, chopped
2 tsp finely chopped garlic
6 eggs
salt and pepper to taste
basil and chives for garnishing

1. Heat 2 tablespoons of oil in a pan and cook the potato slices until soft, then remove and set aside.
2. In the same pan on a low heat, add the balance of the oil, the onions, green pepper and garlic and cook slowly until soft and almost caramelised.
3. While the onion mixture is cooking, whisk the eggs together in a bowl and season generously with salt and pepper.
4. When the onions are ready, add the potatoes and stir together gently.
5. Pour in the eggs and fry gently until almost cooked and starting to brown on the edges.
6. To cook the tortilla on the other side, place a plate on top of the pan, flip the pan over so that the tortilla is on the plate and then gently slide the tortilla back into the pan. Don't overcook the tortilla as you want it to remain a little soft in the middle.
7. Slide the tortilla onto a serving plate and cool slightly before cutting into slices. Garnish with basil and chives, and serve.

BREAKFAST SLICES

BACON, MUSHROOMS AND MELTED EMMENTAL — OH MY! THESE GORGEOUSLY GOOEY TORTILLA SLICES ARE OOZING WITH FLAVOUR — WHAT MORE COULD YOU WANT FROM A BRUNCH-TIME TREAT? IF YOU ARE A MUSHROOM LOVER, THIS RECIPE IS FOR YOU. ALL TYPES OF EDIBLE MUSHROOMS CONTAIN VARYING DEGREES OF PROTEIN AND FIBRE AS WELL AS A POWERFUL ANTIOXIDANT CALLED SELENIUM, WHICH HELPS TO SUPPORT THE IMMUNE SYSTEM. ANOTHER EASY-TO-MAKE RECIPE, IT CAN BE ON THE TABLE IN LESS THAN 15 MINUTES AND WILL HAVE EVERYONE CLAMOURING FOR A SECOND SLICE AND MAYBE A THIRD.

---

4 stone ground traditional wraps
12 small cherry tomatoes or
    12 slices jalapeño pepper
    for garnishing
12 toothpicks
chopped chives for garnishing

FILLING 1
2 Tbsp butter
1½ cups sliced mushrooms
1 red pepper, finely chopped
4 slices bacon, chopped
½ tsp dried thyme
salt and pepper to taste
1½ cups grated Emmental cheese

FILLING 2
½ tsp finely chopped garlic
½ cup finely chopped onion
1½ cups grated Cheddar cheese

1. To make filling 1, heat the butter in a pan, add the mushrooms, red pepper, bacon and thyme, season with salt and pepper and sauté until the bacon is cooked, the mushrooms have browned and the red pepper has softened. Remove and set aside.
2. To make filling 2, combine the garlic, onion and Cheddar cheese and set aside.
3. Place one wrap into the pan used to make the filling, scatter over the bacon mixture, making sure the whole surface is covered evenly.
4. Scatter over the Emmental cheese, again making sure the whole surface is covered evenly, especially the edges.
5. Place another wrap on top of the mixture and, on a medium heat, brown the base of the bottom wrap, then carefully flip it over and brown the other side. The wraps should start to harden.
6. Once browned, remove and set aside.
7. Place another wrap in the pan, scatter over the Cheddar cheese and onion mixture, making sure the whole surface is covered evenly. Season generously with salt and pepper.
8. Place the last wrap on top of the mixture and, on a medium heat, brown the base of the wrap, then carefully flip it over and brown the other side. Once browned, remove and set aside.
9. Cut each stack into 12 slices. Place the two different fillings on top of each other.
10. Skewer a cherry tomato or a slice of jalapeño pepper onto each toothpick and insert into the double stack of wraps.
11. Finally scatter over some chopped chives. Serve immediately.

CAESAR-STYLE EGGS

AREN'T HARD-BOILED EGGS JUST THE PERFECT UNION WITH CAESAR SALAD? BUT ACTUALLY, THE SECRET TO THIS RECIPE IS ADDING A DASH OF ANCHOVY PASTE TO GIVE THEM THAT CAESAR-STYLE DRESSING. ANCHOVIES ARE A GOOD SOURCE OF VITAMIN B, SUCH AS THIAMIN, RIBOFLAVIN, NIACIN AND FOLATE, AS WELL AS VITAMIN K, SO THIS SAUCY LITTLE SECRET MEANS YOUR EGGS GET A SNEAKY DOSE OF EXTRA NUTRITION. THIS RECIPE TURNS RUN-OF-THE-MILL DEVILLED EGGS INTO AN APPETISER THAT'S RICH AND ELEGANT, WITH THE ADDED BENEFIT OF BEING EASY TO FEED A CROWD.

5 large eggs, hard boiled and peeled
3 slices streaky bacon
1 Tbsp lemon juice
3 spring onions, chopped for garnishing
1 Tbsp grated Parmesan cheese for garnishing

CAESAR DRESSING
¼ cup mayonnaise
½ tsp finely chopped garlic
1 Tbsp anchovy paste
1 Tbsp lemon juice
½ tsp Dijon mustard
½ tsp Worcestershire sauce
½ cup finely grated Parmesan cheese
salt and pepper to taste

1. Slice the eggs in half and remove the egg yolks, setting both the yolks and the egg white halves aside.
2. In a pan, fry the bacon until crisp, then remove and place on paper towel to absorb any excess oil. Finely chop the bacon and set aside.
3. To make the dressing, in a bowl whisk the mayonnaise, garlic, anchovy paste, lemon juice, mustard and Worcestershire sauce.
4. Mash the cooked egg yolks and add to the dressing together with the cheese. Season with salt and pepper, then stir to ensure that the ingredients are well combined.
5. Stir in half the bacon pieces and the lemon juice.
6. Spoon the mixture into the egg white halves. If necessary, slice a small piece off the bottom of the eggs so that they balance evenly on the plate.
7. Garnish with the remaining bacon bits, the spring onions and grated Parmesan and serve.

Caesar-style eggs

Breakfast slices

VEGETARIAN

It's a sure way to let down vegetarians – invite them to a party where all they can eat is a lifeless cheese sandwich or a dusty bowl of nuts. It goes without saying that omnivores usually have it much easier when it comes to food choices, but luckily tapas cater for every palate. In fact, many traditional tapas dishes are naturally vegetarian, which is great news for the veggie-vores in your life. Beautiful, flavourful and imaginative, these veggie tapas are anything but boring.

When you need to cater for a large group or particularly fussy eaters, it's always a good idea to serve a few meatless tapas at your gathering. This way there are cool and colourful treats on your party table and no one is left standing hungry. With veggie snacks like caramelised onion and goat's milk cheese tartlets, finger foods like the beetroot and halloumi skewers or the quintessential Spanish gazpacho shooter on offer, these veggie-licious recipes are sure to hit the spot.

Best of all, I love the simplicity of these tapas. You can produce a delicious selection of dishes using simple, fresh, local ingredients which, when paired in an inventive way, show off their individual qualities. Even confirmed meat eaters will be finishing off plates in no time and coming back for another round. So, whether you are entertaining vegetarians or just like having variety on the table, this compilation of vivacious vegetarian tapas dishes is sure to tickle your taste buds.

DIPPED BAKED PRETZELS

ALL YOU NEED ARE A FEW INGREDIENTS TO MAKE THESE WARM, BUTTERY PRETZELS. GOLDEN, WITH A SOFT CHEWY INTERIOR AND A SALTY EXTERIOR, THESE TWISTED BEAUTIES ARE DESIGNED TO BE DIPPED.

1½ cups warm water
1 tsp salt
1 Tbsp brown sugar
480g cake wheat flour
1 large egg, beaten
coarse sea salt, for sprinkling

BEER & MUSTARD DIP
1 cup beer
8 tsp brown sugar
2–3 Tbsp hot mustard
⅓ cup Dijon mustard

CHEESE & JALAPEÑO DIP
¼ cup cream cheese
2 Tbsp sour cream
8 tsp finely diced jalapeños
  (sweet, from a jar)
4 tsp jalapeño juice
  (from the jar)
½ cup finely grated Cheddar
  cheese

ONION DIP
2 Tbsp vegetable oil
1 onion, finely sliced
¼ cup water
1 cup dry white wine
2 chicken stock cubes
2 bay leaves
1 tsp dried thyme
½ cup sour cream
¼ cup creamy mayonnaise
1 tsp Worcestershire sauce
salt and pepper to taste

1. To make the beer & mustard dip, heat the beer and sugar in a saucepan and allow to simmer until about a third of the beer has reduced and the sugar granules have dissolved.
2. Stir in the mustards and simmer for a few more minutes.
3. Remove, cool and store in an airtight container in the fridge until ready to serve.
4. To make the cheese & jalapeño dip, combine all the ingredients and store in the fridge until ready to serve.
5. To make the onion dip, add the oil and onion to a saucepan and cook for about 10 minutes, stirring often until the onion is soft.
6. Add the water, wine, stock cubes, bay leaf and thyme and bring to the boil. Reduce the heat and allow to simmer for about 10 minutes or until most of the liquid has reduced.
7. Using a slotted spoon, remove the onion and place in a separate bowl.
8. To the onions, add the remaining ingredients and, using a stick blender, blitz until the onion is diced and the sauce is well combined. Refrigerate until ready to use.
9. To make the pretzels, preheat the oven to 215°C and line a baking sheet with baking paper.

10. Combine the water, salt and sugar in a mixing bowl. Slowly add the flour, one cup at a time, and mix with a wooden spoon until the dough is thick. If it is still sticky, add more flour until the dough bounces back when you poke it.
11. Knead the dough for about 3 minutes and shape into a ball.
12. Break off pieces of dough that are roughly the size of the pretzel you want to make. For mini ones, a 5cm-diameter ball of dough should be sufficient.
13. Roll each ball into a rope and twist into a pretzel shape.
14. Brush the pretzels with the beaten egg. Place them onto the baking sheet and sprinkle with salt.
15. Bake for 7–10 minutes. They should be nice and brown, but if you want them a little crispier, you can grill the tops a little to finish them off.
16. Cool and serve with the various dips.

BEETROOT & HALLOUMI SKEWERS

THERE'S ALWAYS SOMETHING SO TEMPTING ABOUT EATING FOOD ON A STICK. THESE MARINATED BEETROOT AND HALLOUMI SKEWERS ARE NO EXCEPTION. BEST OF ALL, THIS RECIPE IS A QUICK AND EASY WAY TO ADD EXTRA FLAVOUR AND COLOUR, CREATING A SERIOUSLY YUMMY SNACK. SERVED ON A PRETTY ROSEMARY SKEWER, THESE ARE THE PERFECT OPTION FOR KEEPING VEGETARIANS HAPPY. BEST OF ALL, THEY'RE A GREAT HEALTH CHOICE TOO AS BEETROOT IS HIGH IN SEVERAL BENEFICIAL PLANT COMPOUNDS WHICH ARE ASSOCIATED WITH REDUCING BLOOD PRESSURE.

12 rosemary sprigs to use as skewers
¼ cup lemon juice
½ cup olive oil
2 Tbsp chopped fresh thyme leaves
2 Tbsp chopped fresh parsley
1 clove garlic, finely chopped
salt and pepper to taste (halloumi can be quite salty so use salt with caution)
200g halloumi cheese
4 medium beetroot
2 Tbsp balsamic vinegar
1 tsp Dijon mustard
2 spring onions, finely chopped

1. Soak the rosemary sprigs in cold water for at least half an hour to stop them from burning.
2. In a blender, blitz the lemon juice, half of the olive oil, the thyme, parsley, garlic, salt and pepper, then set aside.
3. Pat the halloumi dry and cut into 2cm x 2cm cubes. Place in a dish and pour over the herb marinade. Cover the cheese and refrigerate until ready to use.
4. Peel, top and tail the beetroot and cut into cubes about the same size as the cheese.
5. Bring some water to the boil and cook the beetroot cubes until cooked but still firm. Drain and set aside.
6. In a bowl, combine the vinegar, mustard and spring onions and blend well.
7. Slowly whisk in the remaining olive oil.
8. Pour the mixture over the cooked beetroot and set aside for about 15 minutes.
9. Thread the halloumi and beetroot alternately onto the rosemary sticks.
10. Cook for 4–5 minutes on each side under the grill (or on a braai if you prefer), until the cheese is browned and crisp on the outside.
11. Drizzle the remaining sauce from the beetroot over the skewers and serve.

BUTTERNUT & GNOCCHI BITES

INDIVIDUAL GNOCCHI MAKE A SURPRISINGLY CLEVER ADDITION TO A TAPAS OFFERING AS THESE PUFFY POTATO MORSELS ARE JUST THE RIGHT SIZE TO POP INTO YOUR MOUTH. THE NATURAL SWEETNESS OF THE BUTTERNUT IS INCREDIBLY APPEALING WHEN PAIRED WITH THE FRIED SAGE AND TOMATO, CREATING TAPAS BURSTING WITH FLAVOUR. MOVE OVER PESTO PASTA, GNOCCHI BITES ARE HERE TO STAY.

---

2 Tbsp soy sauce
2 Tbsp sesame oil
2 Tbsp honey
12–16 butternut cubes
¼ cup sesame seeds, toasted

12–16 gnocchi pieces
6–8 sage leaves
½ tsp olive oil
6–8 sundried tomatoes in olive oil, halved
toothpicks

1. Preheat the oven to 180°C.
2. Combine the soy sauce, sesame oil and honey and pour over the butternut cubes.
3. Place the cubes on a greased baking sheet and bake in the oven until cooked through and softened.
4. Remove and roll in the sesame seeds.
5. Cook the gnocchi according to the packet instructions. Remove and set aside.
6. Fry the sage leaves in the oil until almost crisp, remove and drain on paper towel.
7. To serve, first skewer a sage leaf, then a piece of sundried tomato, a cube of butternut, and finally a piece of gnocchi.

GAZPACHO SHOOTERS

GAZPACHO IS THE QUINTESSENTIAL SUMMER TOMATO SOUP OF SPAIN, ORIGINATING IN ANDALUCIA. IT'S SO POPULAR AND MANY REGIONS HAVE THEIR OWN NAME AND VARIATION OF IT, FROM *SALMOREJO* IN CORDOBA TO *AJOBLANCO* IN GRANADA. BUT THEY ALL HAVE ONE THING IN COMMON: SERVING IT SUPER CHILLED TO KEEP YOU COOL AND REFRESHED DURING THE HOT SUMMER MONTHS.
   INSTEAD OF USING BREAD IN THE SOUP, I'VE OPTED TO USE THE BREAD FOR CHEESY TOASTS – WHAT'S NOT TO LOVE ABOUT MELTED CHEESE AND TOMATO?

¼ cucumber, chopped
1 red pepper, chopped
1 x 400g tin chopped tomatoes
2 Tbsp tomato paste
1 Tbsp Worcestershire sauce
a few drops of Tabasco
   to your liking
½ tsp finely chopped garlic
a pinch of sugar

salt and pepper to taste
½ cup Greek yoghurt
extra Greek yoghurt for
   garnishing (optional)
mint leaves for garnishing

CHEESE TOASTS
4 slices white bread
¼ cup cream cheese

2 Tbsp grated Cheddar
black pepper
1 Tbsp poppy seeds
1 Tbsp sesame seeds
2 tsp onion flakes
2 tsp garlic flakes
1 tsp coarse salt

1. To make the soup, use a stick blender to blitz the cucumber, red pepper and tinned tomatoes.
2. Add the tomato paste, Worcestershire sauce, Tabasco, garlic, sugar, salt and pepper and blend together. Add the yoghurt and give a final blend.
3. Chill until ready to serve.
4. To make the cheese toasts, preheat the oven to 180°C.
5. Cut the crusts off the bread and then slice the bread into 2cm-wide lengths.
6. Place on a baking sheet in the oven and bake for a few minutes until the bread starts to harden.
7. Combine the cream cheese and Cheddar and season generously with pepper.
8. In a separate bowl, combine the poppy seeds and sesame seeds, onion and garlic flakes and salt.
9. Spread the cheese mixture over the toasts and scatter the seed mixture on top and bake in the oven until the cheese starts to melt.
10. Remove and allow to cool slightly. (Any leftover seed mixture can be stored in an airtight container.)
11. Serve the gazpacho in shot glasses with a dollop of yoghurt, if using, and a mint leaf as garnish, with the cheese toasties on the side.

Butternut & gnocchi bites

Gazpacho shooters

CARAMELISED ONION & GOAT'S MILK CHEESE TARTLETS

IMPRESS YOUR GUESTS BY BRINGING OUT THIS DELICIOUS VEGGIE TARTLET MADE FROM SCRATCH. CREAMY GOAT'S MILK CHEESE AND SWEET CARAMELISED ONIONS ARE BAKED ON TOP OF THE PASTRY WITH THYME, TRUFFLE OIL AND BALSAMIC GLAZE. GOAT'S MILK CHEESE IS HEALTHIER THAN THE CHEESE MADE FROM COW'S MILK AS IT HAS LESS LACTOSE, LOWER SODIUM AND EASIER-TO-DIGEST FATS. IT ALSO CONTAINS MORE PROBIOTICS, PERFECT FOR GUT HEALTH. THESE TINY TARTS ARE A TRUE VEGETARIAN DELIGHT.

2 onions, sliced
2 Tbsp butter
2 Tbsp sugar
2 tsp chopped fresh thyme
a pinch of salt
1 x 400g packet ready rolled puff pastry
100g goat's milk cheese
9 drops white truffle oil
1 Tbsp balsamic glaze
extra thyme for garnishing

1. Preheat the oven to 180°C.
2. In a pot, gently sauté the onions in the butter for 5–7 minutes.
3. Stir in the sugar and thyme and season with salt. Continue to cook for a further 5–7 minutes until the onions have caramelised and turned golden.
4. Roll out the puff pastry and cut out circles using a 6cm or 7cm cookie cutter.
5. Grease a muffin tin and place the pastry circles into the muffin holes. Prick the pastry circles with a fork.
6. Add about 1 teaspoon of onion mixture to each muffin hole, followed by a slice of goat's milk cheese.
7. Place in the oven and bake for about 15 minutes or until the pastry has turned golden.
8. Remove and allow to cool slightly.
9. Stir the truffle oil into the balsamic glaze.
10. To serve, add 1 teaspoon of onion mixture to each tartlet, drizzle over the truffle glaze and scatter with fresh thyme.

CARROT & PEA TRIANGLES

THESE TRIANGLES ARE A DELICIOUS AND HEALTHY ALTERNATIVE TO THE TRADITIONAL SAMOOSA AS THEY USE PHYLLO PASTRY AND ARE BAKED IN THE OVEN – WHICH MEANS A LOT LESS FAT THAN FRYING. CARROTS ARE AN EXCELLENT SOURCE OF VITAMIN A, WHILE GREEN PEAS ARE FILLING DUE TO THE HIGH AMOUNTS OF PROTEIN AND FIBRE THEY CONTAIN, WHICH MEANS YOU'LL FEEL FULL AND CONTENT. BEAUTIFULLY CRISP AND FLAKY, THESE VIBRANT VEGGIE PARCELS ARE A CONFIDENT CROWD-PLEASER.

2–3 medium carrots
salt and pepper to taste
¼ tsp olive oil
¼ tsp honey
100g frozen baby peas
2 spring onions,
   finely chopped

80g cream cheese
100g Parmesan cheese,
   finely grated
3 sheets phyllo pastry
about 5 tsp melted butter
   for brushing

GLUE
¼ cup cake wheat flour
¼ cup water

1. Preheat the oven to 180°C and line a baking sheet with baking paper.
2. Peel and cut the carrots into small cubes.
3. Place the carrots on the prepared baking sheet and toss with salt, olive oil and honey.
4. Roast for 10–15 minutes until tender, remove from the oven and set aside to cool.
5. In a pot over a medium heat, simmer the peas in a little water for 3 minutes, then drain.
6. In a bowl, combine the peas, carrots, spring onion, cream cheese and Parmesan cheese and season well with salt and pepper.
7. Line the baking sheet with a clean sheet of baking paper.
8. Lay the sheets of phyllo on a large board and cut them into 8cm-wide strips across the width of the phyllo sheets.
9. Make the glue by mixing the flour and water to form a paste.
10. Place about a teaspoon of the pea and carrot mixture onto the bottom left-hand corner of each strip of phyllo.
11. Fold the right-hand corner of the phyllo over the filling, towards the left-hand side, to form a triangle that just covers the filling. Then take the small triangle and flip it to the other side and continue flipping until you have used up all the pastry. Leave the last triangular piece open. Using your finger, gently dab some glue over the last piece of pastry and stick it down to seal. If there are any holes in the corners, you can use the glue to stick the phyllo sheets together.
12. Brush all the triangles on both sides with the melted butter and place on the baking sheet.
13. Bake in the oven for about 10 minutes, flip them over and continue to bake for another 5 minutes, or until the triangles are golden.
14. Remove and set aside, then serve once cool enough to handle.

FLAVOURED CHEESE STRAWS

NO PARTY WOULD BE COMPLETE WITHOUT CHEESE STRAWS. BUT THESE AREN'T THE PLAIN OLD CHEESE STRAWS YOU WOULD NORMALLY EXPECT ON A TABLE AS THESE HAVE SOME INTERESTING FILLINGS. WE'RE ALL FAMILIAR WITH BASIL PESTO, BUT WHAT ABOUT THE MORE UNUSUAL CORIANDER PESTO, AND WHO WOULD HAVE THOUGHT TO PLACE IT IN A CHEESE STRAW? BUT THE END RESULT IS DEFINITELY MORE-ISH. THE SAME GOES WITH CHEESE AND CHUTNEY — OH WOW! WHAT A DELICIOUS COMBINATION. FINALLY, CUMIN SEEDS ARE A PERFECT MATCH FOR CHEDDAR, SO WHY NOT PUT THEM INTO A STRAW? WITHOUT A DOUBT, THESE SUPER TASTY SNACKS WILL PROVE TO BE UNBELIEVABLY POPULAR.

1 x 400g packet ready rolled puff pastry
melted butter for brushing

CHEESE & CHUTNEY FILLING
¾ cup grated Cheddar cheese
3 Tbsp chutney

CORIANDER PESTO FILLING
2½ Tbsp coriander pesto
¾ cup grated Cheddar cheese

CUMIN SEEDS FILLING
1½ tsp cumin seeds
¾ cup grated Cheddar cheese

1. Preheat the oven to 190°C.
2. To make the fillings, combine the ingredients of each individually and set aside.
3. Roll out the pastry about 3mm thick and cut into three equal pieces.
4. Spread the cheese and chutney mixture along the length of one of the pieces of pastry, filling only half of the pastry.
5. Fold the other half of the pastry over the mixture and press down. Cut the pastry into 2–2.5cm-wide strips and twist each strip before placing it on a greased baking sheet.
6. Repeat the procedure with the other 2 fillings.
7. Brush the cheese straws with the melted butter and bake in the oven for 12–15 minutes until cooked and golden.

Carrot & pea triangles

Flavoured cheese straws

DAHL IN MINI BREAD BASKETS

IF YOU LOVE LENTILS AS I DO, YOU SIMPLY MUST TRY THIS RECIPE. LENTILS ARE COMFORT FOOD TO ME AND ARE AN EXCELLENT SOURCE OF B VITAMINS, IRON, MAGNESIUM, POTASSIUM AND ZINC. INDIAN RECIPES CAN SOMETIMES BE TRICKY BECAUSE THEY CAN INCLUDE INGREDIENTS THAT YOU DON'T HAVE OR THAT YOU MAY NOT EVEN HAVE HEARD OF BEFORE. THIS RECIPE, ON THE OTHER HAND, IS DIFFERENT. ALTHOUGH THERE ARE MANY SPICES, IT'S SIMPLE, IT'S DELICIOUS AND IT'S SUPER FILLING. A RUSTIC WHOLESOME DISH SERVED UP IN AN ADORABLE EDIBLE BREAD BASKET.

1 Tbsp olive oil
1 onion, finely chopped
1 tsp finely chopped garlic
2 tsp finely chopped ginger
2 tsp ground coriander
2 tsp ground cumin
2 tsp ground turmeric
2 tsp garam masala
¼–½ tsp dried chilli flakes
  (optional)

4 tomatoes, peeled and
  chopped
¼ cup lemon juice
1 x 410g tin brown lentils,
  drained and rinsed
salt and pepper to taste
plain full cream yoghurt for
  garnishing
fresh coriander for garnishing

MINI NAAN BREAD BASKETS
1 cup Greek yoghurt
2 cups self-raising flour
¼ tsp salt

1. Preheat the oven to 190°C.
2. To make the bread baskets, combine the Greek yoghurt, flour and salt in a bowl to form a dough.
3. Tip the dough out onto a floured surface and using a rolling pin, roll the dough out until quite thin, about 2mm thick.
4. Turn a small muffin tin over and grease the under sides of each muffin hole.
5. Cut out dough circles big enough to fit over the upturned muffin holders. I use a 7cm cookie cutter. Drape the dough over each upturned holder and gently pat around the holder to ensure it fits, then cut off any excess dough. Continue until you have used up all the dough.
6. Place the muffin tin in the oven and bake for about 10 minutes or until the baskets turn golden.
7. Remove the muffin tin from the oven and allow to cool. Once cool enough to handle, remove the bread baskets from the muffin tin and set aside until ready to use.

8. To make the lentil dahl, heat the oil in a pan, fry the onions for a few minutes, then add the garlic, ginger, coriander, cumin, turmeric, garam masala and chilli flakes, if using, and fry until the onion has softened.

9. Add the tomatoes and continue to cook for about 5 minutes. Stir in the lemon juice.

10. Finally add the lentils, season with salt and pepper and mix to ensure that all the ingredients are well combined and heated through.

11. Spoon the lentil dahl into the mini naan bread baskets, garnish with a spoonful of yoghurt and a coriander leaf and serve immediately.

MINI RICE CAKES WITH HUMMUS & PICKLED CARROT

HUMMUS IS BECOMING MORE AND MORE POPULAR AND FOR GOOD REASON. THIS MIDDLE EASTERN SPECIALITY IS FULL OF GOODNESS AND FLAVOUR THANKS TO THE HUMBLE CHICKPEA. PICKLING FOOD IS ALSO GAINING IN POPULARITY AS THIS CAN HELP WITH EVERYTHING FROM INSULIN RESISTANCE TO IMFLAMMATION. I LOVE THE CREAMY SOFT TEXTURE OF THE HUMMUS AGAINST THE TANGY ALMOST SOUR TASTE OF THE PICKLED CARROT. SERVED ON FLAVOURED MINI RICE CAKES, THEY MAKE THE PERFECT PLANT-POWERED PARTY SNACK IN A FLASH.

¾ cup hummus
12–14 cheese-flavoured mini rice cakes
18–21 raisins, halved
micro herbs for garnishing

PICKLED CARROTS
1 Tbsp sugar
1 Tbsp white wine vinegar
2 Tbsp water
1–2 medium carrots, shaved into ribbons

1. To make the pickled carrots, combine the sugar, vinegar and water.
2. Add the carrot ribbons to the pickling juice and allow to marinate for about half an hour.
3. To serve, place a tablespoon of hummus onto each mini rice cake, top with a ribbon or two of the pickled carrot and about 3 pieces of raisin.
4. Garnish with micro herbs and serve immediately.

PITA FRIES WITH ZA'ATAR & FETA

EXTRA CRISP, EXTRA GOLDEN AND EXTRA DELICIOUS, THIS PITA RECIPE WILL QUICKLY BECOME YOUR NEWEST FAVOURITE. A SUPER SIMPLE RECIPE THAT IS BROUGHT TO LIFE WITH THE ADDITION OF ZA'ATAR. IF YOU'RE NOT FAMILIAR WITH ZA'ATAR, IT'S A FLAVOURFUL MIDDLE EASTERN SPICE BLEND THAT INCLUDES SUMAC. SUMAC IS ONE OF THE MOST POWERFUL ANTI-INFLAMMATORY SPICES OUT THERE, MADE FROM RUBY-COLOURED BERRIES, WHICH ARE GROUND INTO A BEAUTIFUL, COARSE POWDER THAT BURSTS WITH COLOUR AND FLAVOUR. IT'S GORGEOUS AND HEALTHY. COMBINED WITH CREAMY FETA CHEESE, THESE PITA FRIES ARE FIT FOR A KING.

4–6 mini pitas
olive oil for drizzling
½–¾ cup crumbled feta

ZA'ATAR SPICE
½ tsp roasted sesame seeds
1 tsp dried thyme
1 tsp dried origanum
2 Tbsp sumac
½ tsp coarse salt

1. Preheat the oven to 180°C.
2. To make the za'atar spice, combine all the spice ingredients and use a pestle and mortar to pound all the ingredients until they have broken up.
3. Slice the mini pitas in half horizontally and then slice into quarters.
4. Drizzle some olive oil over the pita slices and generously season with the za'atar spice.
5. Finally scatter over the feta cheese, place in the oven and bake for 5–7 minutes or until the pitas turn golden.
6. Remove and eat while still warm.

SUSHI TOASTIES

IT'S TIME TO COMBINE TWO FAVOURITE CULINARY CONCEPTS. AS THE NAME SUGGESTS, THIS RECIPE IS THE LOVE CHILD OF A WESTERN SANDWICH AND A JAPANESE SUSHI ROLL. I LOVE ALL THE FLAVOURS OF SUSHI, BUT DON'T FANCY ALL THE WORK. SO, THIS RECIPE GIVES ME MY VEGETARIAN SUSHI FIX IN A CLEVER AND EASY WAY, PLUS IT'S MUCH MORE ECONOMICAL THAN BUYING SUSHI.

5–6 slices white bread
3 Tbsp tangy mayonnaise
3 Tbsp cream cheese
1 Tbsp finely chopped pickled ginger
toasted sesame seeds for garnishing
10–12 pieces pickled ginger
10–12 slices cucumber
chopped chives or crisp nori for garnishing

CRISP NORI
2 sheets nori (seaweed sheets)
1½ tsp olive oil
salt

1. To make the crisp nori, preheat the oven to 150°C.
2. Place the nori, smooth side down, on a greased baking sheet.
3. Lightly brush the olive oil over the sheets, season with salt and bake in the oven until the nori is dry and crisp, 3–4 minutes. Once crisp, break into pieces.
4. Cut the crusts off the bread and use a cookie cutter to cut out two circles from each slice of bread.
5. Place the bread circles on a baking sheet and place under a grill until just starting to harden. You don't want to make it too toasted.
6. Combine the mayonnaise, cream cheese and chopped pickled ginger.
7. To serve, spread a teaspoon or two of the mayo and cream cheese mixture onto each toast, sprinkle over some sesame seeds, add a slice of pickled ginger and a slice of cucumber and finish off with a few chopped chives or crisp nori.

Pita fries with za'atar & feta

Sushi toasties

VEGETABLE LAYER CAKE

IT'S IMPORTANT TO GET LOTS OF COLOUR ON YOUR TAPAS TABLE AND THIS SAVOURY VEGETABLE CAKE DEFINITELY DOES THE JOB. ALTHOUGH IT MIGHT BE A BIT MORE WORK, WITH FOUR FILLINGS AND A TART TOMATO RELISH, IT'S WORTH IT BECAUSE THIS TAPAS IS BURSTING WITH JUICY, VEGGIE GOODNESS. EACH LAYER IN THIS STACK HAS ITS OWN NUTRITIONAL OOMPH BUT SPINACH IS THE STAR OF THIS SHOW WITH ITS SUPER HIGH IRON CONTENT, WHICH IS GREAT FOR TREATING ANAEMIA, FOR EYE HEALTH AND BLOOD PRESSURE. JAM-PACKED WITH NUTRITIOUS VEG, THIS IS ONE CAKE YOU DON'T NEED TO FEEL GUILTY ABOUT EATING.

5 flour tortillas
2–3 tsp Greek yoghurt
1 cup grated Cheddar cheese

LEEK FILLING
1 Tbsp olive oil
6 small leeks, finely chopped
¼ red onion, finely chopped
1 Tbsp butter
¼ tsp dried thyme
salt and pepper to taste

MUSHROOM FILLING
3 cups chopped mushrooms
¼ tsp dried thyme
2 Tbsp butter
salt and pepper to taste

BABY MARROW FILLING
2 cups chopped baby marrow
¼ tsp dried thyme
1 Tbsp olive oil
salt and pepper to taste

SPINACH FILLING
4 cups roughly chopped spinach
1 Tbsp olive oil
a pinch of nutmeg
1 Tbsp Greek yoghurt
salt and pepper to taste

TOMATO RELISH
½ x 400g tin chopped tomatoes
1 tsp sugar
salt and pepper to taste

1. To make the leek filling, add the olive oil to a pan, add the leeks and onion and sauté gently.
2. After a few minutes, add the butter and thyme and continue to sauté until the leeks and onion have softened. Season with salt and pepper. Remove and set aside.
3. To make the mushroom filling, use the same pan you used for the leeks and gently sauté the mushrooms and thyme in the butter until the mushrooms are soft. Season with salt and pepper. Remove and set aside.
4. To make the baby marrow filling, using the same pan, gently sauté the baby marrow and thyme in the olive oil, until softened. Season with salt and pepper. Remove and set aside.
5. To make the spinach filling, add the spinach leaves, a pinch of nutmeg and olive oil to the same pan and sauté gently until the leaves just start to wilt. Stir in the Greek yoghurt and salt and pepper. Remove and set aside.

6. To make the tomato relish, add the chopped tomatoes, sugar, salt and pepper to a separate pan and cook on medium to high heat until the tomato mixture has reduced and softened. Remove from the heat and set aside.

7. To prepare the tortillas, wipe out any leftover liquid from the spinach, then place one tortilla at a time in the pan and toast both sides until golden.

8. To assemble, place a tortilla on a greased baking sheet and spread the Greek yoghurt over it.

9. Add the mushrooms, spreading the mixture all the way to the edges.

10. Top with another tortilla and spread the wilted spinach all the way to the edges.

11. Continue with the leeks and baby marrow mixtures, topping each layer with a tortilla.

12. Spread the tomato mixture over the final tortilla and scatter over the grated cheese.

13. Place the tortilla cake under the grill until the cheese has melted and turned golden.

14. Remove, allow to cool slightly, then slice into wedges, garnish and serve while still warm.

CUCUMBER RIBBONS WITH FETA & OLIVE SPREAD

EVERY TIME I POP ONE OF THESE INTO MY MOUTH, I'M TRANSPORTED STRAIGHT TO A TAVERNA ON A GREEK ISLAND. WHAT COULD BE MORE GREEK THAN OLIVES, YOGHURT AND FETA? GREEK SALAD FLAVOURS ARE CREATED WHEN THE CRUMBLY FETA IS TRANSFORMED INTO A CREAMY MIXTURE WITH THE SALTY, BRINY OLIVES. A DASH OF OIL, A SPRINKLING OF ORIGANUM AND YOU HAVE YOURSELF A GREEK MARVEL, ALL ROLLED INTO A CUCUMBER RIBBON. BEST OF ALL, YOU CAN MAKE THE DIP A COUPLE OF DAYS BEFOREHAND AND ASSEMBLE JUST BEFORE SERVING.

200g feta cheese
½ cup Greek yoghurt
1 clove garlic, finely chopped
2 Tbsp olive oil
1½ tsp dried origanum
4 pitted green olives
½ tsp lemon juice
10–12 cucumber ribbons

1. Add all the ingredients, except the cucumber, to a blender and blitz together.
2. Spread the cucumber ribbons with the whipped feta mixture and roll up.

STUFFED ARTICHOKES WITH CARAMELISED ONIONS

WE OFTEN ASSOCIATE CARAMELISED ONIONS WITH BURGERS, BUT I'VE TEAMED THEM HERE WITH ARTICHOKES AND BUTTER BEANS TO CREATE A DELIGHTFUL VEGAN SNACK. USING WHITE BALSAMIC VINEGAR STOPS THE ONIONS FROM DARKENING TOO MUCH AND PROVIDES A GENTLER FLAVOUR COMPARED WITH ITS BROWN-HUED COUNTERPART. BUT IF YOU DON'T HAVE ANY WHITE BALSAMIC, THEN THE MORE REGULAR, DARK ONE IS EQUALLY DELICIOUS. BOTH ARE MADE FROM GRAPES, SO YOU CAN'T GO WRONG!

- 1 x 400g tin butter beans
- 2 Tbsp liquid from butter beans
- 3 Tbsp roughly chopped fresh basil
- 1 Tbsp lemon juice

- ¼ cup olive oil
- salt and pepper to taste
- 2 large onions, halved and thinly sliced
- ¼ cup olive oil

- 3 Tbsp white balsamic vinegar
- 3 tsp sugar
- 2 x 390g tins artichoke bottoms or hearts
- micro herbs for garnishing

1. In a blender, whizz the butter beans, 2 Tbsp of liquid from the butter beans, basil leaves, lemon juice and olive oil until puréed. Season with salt and pepper and set aside.
2. In a pot on a low heat, combine the onions, olive oil, balsamic vinegar and sugar and simmer for 15–20 minutes, stirring occasionally, until the onions have softened and caramelised. When cooked, drain off the liquid.
3. If using artichoke hearts, cut them in half.
4. To serve, add a dollop or two of the butter bean purée to each artichoke, add a generous helping of onion and garnish with micro herbs.

PEPPADEW PINTXOS

THIS IS A TRUE BLEND OF SPANISH AND SOUTH AFRICAN CULTURES, WITH A UNIQUELY SOUTH AFRICAN INGREDIENT, THE TANGY PEPPADEW. IT CERTAINLY PACKS A PUNCH, BUT MIXED WITH CHEESE AND SPREAD ON A BAGUETTE, YOU'VE CREATED A DELIGHTFUL PINTXO THAT WOULD SIT PERFECTLY AT HOME NESTLED AMONGST THE VAST ARRAY OF FLAVOURFUL TREATS FOUND ON PINTXOS COUNTERS IN PICTURESQUE SAN SEBASTIAN.

4 Peppadews, finely chopped
2 tsp Peppadew liquid
125g cream cheese
12 slices French baguette
12 slices yellow pepper
pea shoots or baby leaves for garnishing
24 stuffed olives, store bought
toothpicks

1. Combine the chopped Peppadews, Peppadew liquid and cream cheese.
2. Lightly toast the bread.
3. Spread the Peppadew cream generously over the toasted bread slices.
4. Place a slice of yellow pepper on top of the cheese and scatter over the pea shoots or baby leaves.
5. Spear 2 olives on each toothpick and insert into each toast and serve.

CHEESY HERB MUFFINS WITH PEPPADEW CREAM

EVERYONE ENJOYS A CHEESE MUFFIN. BUT I'VE UPPED THE ANTE BY ADDING HERBS TO THE MIX. THE PARSLEY PROVIDES SOME GREENERY WHILE THE DRIED HERBS CARRY THE FLAVOUR. THE PEPPADEWS ADD SOME TANG AND THE APPLE BRINGS THE CRUNCH. PUT THESE ALL TOGETHER AND YOU'VE GOT DELICIOUS, CREAMY MOUTHFULS OF FLAVOUR. BEST OF ALL, THIS RECIPE WILL MAKE 20–25 MINI MUFFINS, SO YOU CAN FREEZE THE EXTRAS FOR ANOTHER TIME.

PEPPADEW CREAM
8 Peppadews
125g cream cheese
2 Tbsp Peppadew liquid

CHEESE & HERB MUFFINS
2 cups flour
3 tsp baking powder
1 tsp salt

1 tsp dried mixed herbs
⅓ cup roughly chopped fresh parsley
1 cup grated Cheddar cheese
1 egg
⅓ cup oil
1 cup milk

1 green apple, skin on and cubed

1. Preheat the oven to 200°C.
2. To make the muffins, sift together the flour, baking powder and salt.
3. Mix in the dried herbs, parsley and cheese.
4. In a separate bowl, combine the egg, oil and milk and add to the dry ingredients.
5. Mix until just combined.
6. Using a mini muffin tin, spoon about a teaspoon of mixture into each holder, filling it up three-quarters of the way, as they will rise during cooking.
7. Bake in the oven for 10–15 minutes or until cooked and golden brown.
8. To make the peppadew cream, finely chop the Peppadews and add to the cream cheese together with the Peppadew liquid.
9. To assemble, cut the muffins in half, spread some peppadew cream on the bottom half, add the cubed apple, then replace the tops.

FISH & SEAFOOD

The Mediterranean region boasts one of the most stunning coastlines in the world, which is why it's the first place I think of whenever the subject of fish tapas comes up. It's the land of olives, goat's milk cheese and sumptuous fresh fish. From sea-bass and tuna to calamari and prawns, it's easy to see why this astonishing array of aquatic creatures and seafood are the stars of so many tapas recipes. South Africa is equally blessed with a rich and diverse coastline, providing us with a wide selection of our own fish and seafood to choose from.

For some people, fish and seafood are something they eat only when going out, as they find them intimidating and bewildering to cook. If this is your perception, then I've got great news for you. There is no need to worry about that when preparing these recipes as they show how beautiful fish can be, without being too fussy and difficult to master.

Fish is also a wonderfully diet-friendly food as it's super low in fat. It doesn't only have a positive impact on your waistline, but also on your liver, brain, and even your sleep. So, if you want to incorporate more fish and seafood into your diet, then this tapas section is the way to go.

You can enjoy any of these fishy snacks as a starter before a meal or make them all at once and savour an array of ocean flavours in one sitting. I find that sharing food tends to make one so much more adventurous, and these fish and seafood tapas recipes are interesting enough that even your most fussy eaters will end up finishing their plate and looking for more.

From smoky snoek pâté to tempting tahini tuna-stuffed peppers, this section offers a variety of tasty snacks sure to please every palate. Best served accompanied by a few friends, some cheery chatting and a refreshing beverage.

PEPPER-CRUSTED TUNA WITH WASABI MAYO

BEING A SUSHI LOVER, I JUST HAD TO INCLUDE A SEARED TUNA RECIPE. WHILE WE ALL LIKE EATING TASTY FOOD, IT'S IMPORTANT TO ENSURE THAT IT'S HEALTHY TOO. TUNA HAS THE BEST OF BOTH, PROVIDING GREAT FLAVOUR WHILE BALANCING CALORIES SINCE IT'S LOW IN FAT AND RICH IN PROTEINS. THE WASABI MAYONNAISE TRULY BRINGS OUT THE BEST IN THE TUNA, PROVIDING A SAVOURY TOUCH WITH A HINT OF HEAT. THIS RECIPE IS EASY TO MAKE, HAS SUCH AN ELEGANT FLAVOUR AND WHEN BEAUTIFULLY PRESENTED, YOUR GUESTS WILL THINK YOU WORKED ON IT FOR HOURS.

1 Tbsp honey
1 Tbsp soy sauce
1 Tbsp dry sherry (optional)
1 Tbsp sesame oil
200g fresh tuna steaks
80g spring onions
2 tsp finely chopped garlic

2 Tbsp olive oil
cracked black pepper
6 baby potatoes, cooked
toothpicks
⅓ cup shredded baby spinach
extra spring onion, sliced on
the diagonal, to garnish

WASABI MAYO
3 Tbsp mayonnaise
2 Tbsp wasabi paste

1. In a bowl, combine the honey, soy sauce, sherry (if using) and sesame oil to create a marinade.
2. Place the tuna steaks in the marinade and refrigerate for 15–30 minutes.
3. While the tuna is marinating, finely slice the spring onions on the diagonal, place them in a lightly heated pan, add the garlic and 1 tablespoon of the olive oil and sauté on a gentle heat until the spring onion has softened. Remove and set aside.
4. Remove the tuna steaks from the marinade and generously coat the steak on both sides with the cracked black pepper.
5. In the same pan you used for the spring onions, add the balance of the olive oil, increase the heat, add the steaks and quickly sear the tuna on both sides until cooked medium rare.
6. Remove the steaks from the pan and bring the leftover marinade to the boil before pouring it over the fish. Allow to rest for a few minutes.
7. Combine the wasabi mayo ingredients and set aside.
8. To assemble, slice the cooked baby potatoes in half, cut the tuna into chunky cubes, just big enough to fit on top of the halved potato.
9. Place a cube of tuna on each potato half, add a dollop of wasabi mayo and scatter over some spring onions. Use the toothpicks to anchor the tuna to the potato. Sprinkle over the shredded spinach and serve.

SMOKED MUSSEL FISH CAKES WITH THAI GREEN CURRY DRESSING

GET YOUR PAN HOT AND YOUR TASTE BUDS JUMPING WITH THESE MARVELLOUS, MODERNISED MUSSEL FISH CAKES. THE LIGHTLY SPICED THAI GREEN CURRY DRESSING HIGHLIGHTS THE SUBTLE SMOKINESS OF THE MUSSELS, CREATING A TASTE EXPLOSION IN YOUR MOUTH.

**MAKES ABOUT
24 FISH CAKES**

1 Tbsp butter, softened
½ red onion, finely diced
¼ tsp finely chopped garlic
¼ tsp ground ginger
a pinch of mustard powder
1½ Tbsp finely chopped fresh
   coriander
1 x 85g tin smoked mussels,
   drained and diced and oil
   reserved

100g hake, cooked and flaked
2 medium potatoes, peeled,
   cooked and finely diced
1 Tbsp oil reserved from the
   smoked mussels
salt and pepper to taste

COATING

½ cup cake wheat flour
2 eggs
1 cup toasted breadcrumbs
chopped chives and coriander
   for garnishing

**THAI GREEN CURRY
   DRESSING**

¼ cup chopped fresh basil
¼ cup chopped fresh coriander
3 Tbsp lemon juice
½ tsp finely chopped garlic
1 tsp finely chopped ginger
1 tsp ground cumin
2 Tbsp fish sauce
½ cup coconut cream
3 tsp green curry paste
2 Tbsp plain full cream yoghurt

1. Melt the butter in a pan, add the onion, garlic, ginger, mustard powder and fresh coriander and sauté until the onion has softened.
2. Using a blender, blitz the mussels, hake, potatoes, onion mixture and 1 tablespoon of the reserved mussel oil until well combined. Season with salt and pepper. Roll the mixture into bite-size balls.
3. For the coating, place the flour on a flat plate and roll each ball in the flour, coating well.
4. Place the fish cakes on a greased baking sheet and chill in the fridge for about 30 minutes so that they become firmer. Preheat the oven to 200°C.
5. Place the eggs in one bowl and whisk well. Place the breadcrumbs in another bowl.
6. Dip each fish cake into the egg, drain off any excess and then roll in the breadcrumbs, ensuring that each is well covered. Place them back on the baking sheet and bake the fish cakes for about 15 minutes. Remove the sheet, turn the fish cakes over and continue to bake for another 10 minutes. Place under the grill for about 5 minutes or until golden.
7. While the fish cakes are baking, place the dressing ingredients in a blender and whizz until well combined.
8. To serve, place the fish cakes on individual spoons, drizzle generously with the dressing and garnish with chopped chives and coriander.

CALAMARI, CHORIZO & PATATAS BRAVAS

PATATAS BRAVAS IS A CLASSIC TAPAS DISH AND THIS VERSION KICKS THE FLAVOUR PROFILE UP A NOTCH WITH THE ADDITION OF CHORIZO AND CALAMARI, ANOTHER TWO SPANISH STAPLES. ORIGINATING FROM THE IBERIAN PENINSULA, CHORIZO ADDS A DELICIOUS SMOKY HEAT, WHILE CALAMARI PROVIDES THE SWEET SALTY TASTE OF THE SEA, OFFERING ALL THE FLAVOURS OF A CLASSIC MEDITERRANEAN DISH.

400g calamari steaks, cut into bite-size pieces
3 Tbsp olive oil
1 tsp finely chopped garlic
1 tsp finely chopped ginger
2 tsp lemon juice
1 red onion
¼ cup diced chorizo

2 potatoes, unpeeled
½ tsp smoked paprika
1 tsp chilli flakes
1 tsp sherry vinegar
salt and pepper to taste
2 Tbsp fresh thyme for garnishing
lemon slices for serving

1. Marinate the calamari in 2 tablespoons of the olive oil, the garlic, ginger and lemon juice for at least half an hour, or longer if possible.
2. Cut the onion in half and then slice the halves finely.
3. Heat the remaining 1 tablespoon of olive oil in a pan and on medium to low heat, sauté the onion for about 10 minutes or until the onion is soft and almost caramelised.
4. Add the chorizo and continue to sauté.
5. In the meantime, cook the potatoes until soft.
6. Chop the potatoes into bite-size pieces and add to the onion mixture.
7. Add the smoked paprika and chilli flakes and stir everything together. Remove and set aside.
8. Using the same pan, turn the heat to high and flash-fry the calamari until just cooked. Be careful not to overcook it as it can become rubbery.
9. Once cooked, reduce the heat, and stir in the onion and potato mixture.
10. Finally, pour over the sherry vinegar and season with salt and pepper.
11. Stir together and sauté gently until the sherry vinegar has evaporated.
12. Serve warm in small bowls, with a scattering of fresh thyme and lemon slices.

SMOKED SNOEK PÂTÉ ON SEED LOAF

WHEN YOU HAVE A PARTY PLANNED BUT YOU'RE SHORT ON TIME, THIS SNOEK PÂTÉ IS AN EASY WIN. YOU CAN WHIP IT UP IN MERE MINUTES AND IT PACKS AN EXTRA FLAVOUR PUNCH THANKS TO A TASTY SPRINKLING OF CAYENNE PEPPER. THE ONIONS ADD THE CRUNCH, THE SEED LOAF BRINGS EXTRA SUSTENANCE AND THE ARILS ADD TANG. SNOEK IS THE PRIDE OF THE CAPE, AND THIS UNPRETENTIOUS FISH IS A HEALTHY, RELATIVELY CHEAP HIGH-PROTEIN AND LOW-FAT FOOD SOURCE THAT IS HIGH IN 'GOOD' OMEGA-3 FATTY ACIDS. FRESH, LIGHT, TASTY AND HEALTHY, THIS RECIPE TICKS PRETTY MUCH ALL THE BOXES.

6–8 slices seed bread
butter for spreading (optional)
¼ cup pomegranate arils
½ cup ready made crisp onions, store bought
dill fronds for garnishing

SNOEK PÂTÉ
2 cups finely flaked smoked snoek
1 x 250g tub smooth cottage cheese
½ cup cream
1½ Tbsp lemon juice
a pinch of cayenne pepper or more if you like the heat
a pinch of paprika
cracked black pepper

1. To make the snoek pâté, place all the pâté ingredients in a bowl and mix well.
2. Place in the fridge to chill.
3. To serve, generously spread the pâté on the buttered (optional) bread, scatter over the arils and crisp onion pieces and garnish with dill fronds.

Calamari, chorizo
& patatas bravas

Smoked snoek pâté
on seed loaf

SALMON & BABY MARROW SKEWERS

LOOKING FOR A LIGHTER, FRESHER WAY TO BRAAI? SAY HELLO TO SALMON AND BABY MARROW SKEWERS, WHICH ARE EASY TO PREPARE AHEAD OF TIME AND QUICK TO COOK. SINCE COOKED BABY MARROW IS PARTICULARLY HIGH IN VITAMIN A, IT HELPS YOUR EYES STAY SHARP AND SHINY. THESE SKEWERS ARE GREAT FOR PARTIES: ALL THE FLAVOUR OF THE OCEAN AND THE VIBRANT COLOURS MEAN THAT THEY LOOK FANTASTIC WHEN PILED ON A PLATTER. SIMPLE, FRESH AND FABULOUS.

16 wooden skewers
¾ cup olive oil, plus 1 Tbsp for sautéing
2 tsp finely chopped garlic
2 Tbsp chopped fresh thyme
½ cup lemon juice
5–6 baby marrows
400g Norwegian salmon, skin removed

HARISSA SAUCE
½ cup Greek yoghurt
½ cup crème fraîche
4 tsp harissa paste
2 tsp grated lemon zest

chopped chives for garnishing

1. Soak the skewers in water for at least half an hour, to stop them from burning.
2. Combine the ¾ cup of olive oil, the garlic, thyme and lemon juice in a flattish dish.
3. Slice the baby marrow into ribbons (I use a potato peeler).
4. Cut the salmon into bite-size pieces.
5. Add the baby marrow and salmon to the lemon and olive oil mixture and let the flavours develop for about half an hour.
6. Thread a ribbon of baby marrow onto a skewer, followed by a piece of salmon and continue alternating until there are 2 pieces of each on a skewer.
7. Heat a pan or place on the braai and cook the skewers, turning them until the salmon has just cooked. Be careful not to overcook the salmon. Remove and set aside.
8. Combine the harissa sauce ingredients and garnish with the chopped chives. Serve with the skewers.

TUNA-STUFFED PEPPER PINTXOS

IT SOUNDS COMPLICATED, BUT IT COMES TOGETHER IN A FLASH WITH CANNED TUNA AND A SURPRISINGLY SIMPLE AND FLAVOURFUL LEMON TAHINI DRESSING. IF YOU'RE NOT ALREADY FAMILIAR WITH TAHINI, IT'S BASICALLY SESAME SEEDS THAT HAVE BEEN GROUND DOWN INTO SESAME SEED BUTTER. IT'S VERY POPULAR IN MEDITERRANEAN AND MIDDLE EASTERN COOKING. THE FLAVOUR IS NUTTY AND EARTHY AND TAHINI IS A GREAT SOURCE OF PHOSPHORUS AND MANGANESE, BOTH OF WHICH ARE IMPORTANT FOR BONE HEALTH. CREAMY WITH A TOUCH OF HEAT, THESE PINTXOS WILL QUICKLY BECOME ONE OF YOUR STANDBYS FOR JUST ABOUT ANY GATHERING.

---

12 snacking peppers
2 x 170g tins tuna in water, drained
¼ cup Greek yoghurt
1 Tbsp capers, halved
15 drops Tabasco or more if you prefer
2 Tbsp finely chopped parsley
3 Tbsp tahini

1 Tbsp lemon juice
salt and pepper to taste
butter for spreading
12 slices French baguette, toasted
crème fraîche for garnishing (optional)
fresh dill and basil sprigs for garnishing

1. Arrange the peppers on a baking sheet and place under the grill, turning once, until the skins start to bubble. Don't let them char. Remove from the grill and allow to cool.
2. Cut off the tops and remove any seeds, but reserve the tops.
3. Combine the tuna, yoghurt, capers, Tabasco, parsley, tahini and lemon juice and season generously with salt and pepper.
4. Butter each slice of toasted bread.
5. To serve, stuff each pepper with the tuna mixture, replacing the reserved top. Place a pepper on top of each slice of toast and garnish with a dollop of crème fraîche, if using, and fresh dill and basil.

HAKE GOUJONS
WITH A QUARTET OF SAUCES

IF YOU'RE LOOKING FOR A SLIGHTLY MORE ADULT AND SOPHISTICATED VERSION OF FISH FINGERS, LOOK NO FURTHER THAN HAKE GOUJONS WITH THREE SAUCES. HAKE IS OFTEN PERCEIVED AS A BORING FISH, BUT I LOVE IT FOR ITS ADAPTABILITY. A CLASSIC IN GASTRONOMY, THIS FISH IS PACKED WITH MANY NUTRIENTS THAT MOST PEOPLE ARE LACKING, SUCH AS HIGH-QUALITY PROTEIN AND IODINE. THESE CRISP, GOLDEN BITES ARE GREAT FOR ANY OCCASION AND ARE WONDERFULLY LIGHT. WITH A CHOICE OF FOUR SAUCES, THERE'S SOMETHING FOR EVERYBODY TO ENJOY.

12 ready prepared hake
   goujons, store bought
24 toothpicks

BROCCOLI SAUCE
6 Tbsp sour cream
4 tsp lemon juice
2 Tbsp blue cheese
1⅓ cups cooked broccoli florets

LEMON & CAPER SAUCE
3 Tbsp capers
3 Tbsp butter
2 tsp finely chopped garlic

2 Tbsp lemon juice
¼ cup grated lemon zest

CAJUN TOMATO SAUCE
¼ cup tomato sauce
2 Tbsp cream cheese
2 Tbsp creamy mayonnaise
2 tsp Cajun spice
½ tsp cayenne pepper

DILL SAUCE
1 cup loosely packed fresh dill,
   including the stalks
1 cup milk

½ onion, diced
1 bay leaf
60g butter
¼ cup cake wheat flour
1 tsp lemon juice
salt and pepper to taste
dill sprigs for garnishing

1. Bake the goujons according to the packet instructions. Remove, cut each goujon in half and keep warm.
2. To make the broccoli sauce, place all the ingredients (except the extra florets for garnishing) in a bowl and, using a stick blender, blitz until well combined.
3. To make the lemon and caper sauce, drain, rinse and roughly chop the capers.
4. In a pan, melt the butter on a low heat. Add the garlic, lemon juice and zest and capers. Bring to a simmer and cook for just under a minute. Stir, remove and set aside until ready to serve.
5. To make the Cajun tomato sauce, add all the ingredients to a bowl and stir together. Refrigerate until ready to serve.
6. To make the dill sauce, separate the dill fronds from the stalks and chop up the leaves, keeping the stalks to one side.

7. Put the milk, onion, bay leaf and dill stalks into a pot and heat until just boiling.
8. Take off the heat and leave the milk mixture to infuse for 25 minutes, then strain through a sieve. Set the strained milk aside.
9. Melt the butter in a non-stick pan and stir in the flour to create a roux. Add some of the strained milk, stirring until smooth. Continue to add more milk, stirring continuously, until the sauce has thickened. Simmer very gently for 5 minutes.
10. Stir in the chopped dill leaves and lemon juice and season with salt and pepper.
11. When ready to serve, allow each guest to add a dollop of their preferred sauce to a piece of baked fish and skewer with a toothpick.

SALMON ON POTATO SLICES WITH DILL CREAM

I LOVE THIS DISH BECAUSE THESE TAPAS LOOK SO FANCY BUT ARE ACTUALLY VERY EASY TO MAKE. SALMON IS ONE OF MY FAVOURITE FISH TO COOK AND IT'S ONE OF THE MOST NUTRITIOUS FOODS ON THE PLANET. THIS POPULAR FATTY FISH IS LOADED WITH NUTRIENTS AND THE INCREDIBLE OMEGA-3, WHICH HELPS WITH EVERYTHING FROM DEPRESSION TO ASTHMA. TRULY A WONDER FOOD, IT'S ALSO TASTY, VERSATILE AND WIDELY AVAILABLE. THESE SALMON POTATO ROUNDS ARE AN IMPRESSIVE APPETISER WHEN ENTERTAINING A CROWD, AND THE TASTE IS UTTERLY HEAVENLY TOO.

2–3 large potatoes, unpeeled
2 Tbsp olive oil
4 pieces fresh salmon, skin on
salt and pepper to taste
⅔ cup crème fraîche
2 Tbsp sour cream

¼ cup plain full cream yoghurt
¼ cup chopped dill, plus extra fronds for
    garnishing
2 Tbsp lemon juice
12–14 cucumber rounds
about 36 small capers

1. Cook the potatoes in a pot of water until almost done.
2. Remove and when cool enough to handle, cut the potatoes into 12–14 thick slices.
3. Pour the olive oil into a pan and fry the potato slices on both sides until browned and crisp. Remove, drain on paper towel and set aside.
4. Season the salmon steaks with salt and pepper. Heat the same pan and cook the salmon pieces, skin side down, until the skin crisps.
5. Turn and cook the other side until the flesh turns pink. Be careful not to overcook the salmon. Remove and set aside.
6. When cool enough to handle, remove the skin and chop the skin into pieces. Set aside.
7. In a small pot, gently heat the crème fraiche, sour cream, yoghurt, dill and lemon juice and stir together. Don't let it boil. Remove and set aside.
8. To assemble, season the potato slices with salt and pepper. Place a slice of cucumber on top of each potato slice.
9. Break up the salmon and place as many pieces as possible on top of the cucumber. Drizzle the dill cream over the salmon, drop about 2 capers on top of the cream, sprinkle over some of the crispy skin and garnish with the dill fronds. Serve immediately.

YELLOWTAIL CEVICHE

CEVICHE IS MADE FROM RAW FISH 'COOKED' IN CITRUS JUICES. THE TRUE ORIGIN OF THIS DISH IS STILL BEING DEBATED, BUT IT'S THE NATIONAL DISH OF PERU, AND ARCHAEOLOGICAL EVIDENCE DATING BACK ALMOST 2000 YEARS SHOWS SOMETHING RESEMBLING CEVICHE BEING EATEN THERE ALL THOSE YEARS AGO. IT WAS TAKEN TO THE SPANISH COLONIES BUT IS NOW POPULAR INTERNATIONALLY. THE FRESH YELLOWTAIL MARINATED IN THREE KINDS OF CITRUS JUICE WILL DEFINITELY KEEP YOUR CITRATE LEVELS UP AND YOUR IMMUNE SYSTEM STRONG.

400g yellowtail
1 grapefruit
1 lime
½ lemon
½ red pepper, finely chopped
¼ red onion, finely chopped
¼ cup finely chopped cucumber
2 Tbsp chopped fresh coriander, plus extra
   for garnishing

1 large tomato, diced
1 avocado, peeled and chopped
salt and pepper to taste
1 Tbsp olive oil
1 tsp balsamic vinegar
½ tsp chilli flakes, or more if preferred
¼ tsp finely chopped garlic
lime cheeks for garnishing

1. Cut the fish into bite-size pieces.
2. Squeeze the juice of the grapefruit, lime and lemon into a flat bowl.
3. Add the fish, stir to ensure that the fish is well covered and submerged, then cover and place in the fridge to 'cook' for 1 hour. Don't leave it for much longer as the fish will become too acidic.
4. After 1 hour, remove the fish and drain off all the marinade.
5. In the same flat bowl, combine the red pepper, onion, cucumber, coriander, tomato, avocado and drained fish pieces. Season well with salt and pepper.
6. In a separate small bowl, combine the olive oil, vinegar, chilli flakes and garlic and add to the fish mixture. Add more chilli flakes if you like a little extra heat.
7. Gently stir everything together and serve in small bowls with lemon cheeks and extra fresh coriander.

Salmon on potato slices
with dill cream

Yellowtail ceviche

RED PEPPER PESTO & CORN SALSA MUSSELS

MUSSELS HAVE THREE THINGS GOING FOR THEM: THEY'RE CHEAP, QUICK TO COOK AND DELICIOUS. THEY'RE ALSO A REGULAR FEATURE ON THE TAPAS TABLES AND PINTXOS COUNTERS IN SPAIN. THIS RECIPE PAIRS THEM UP WITH THE HOLY GRAIL OF PESTOS — RED PEPPER PESTO. THE PESTO IS FRESH AND BRIGHT, BUT IT'S THE CORN SALSA THAT REALLY STEALS THE SHOW. CORN IS RICH IN VITAMIN B_{12}, FOLIC ACID AND IRON, WHICH HELPS IN THE PRODUCTION OF RED BLOOD CELLS IN THE BODY, MAKING IT A WONDERFUL FIX FOR THOSE SUFFERING FROM ANAEMIA. YOUR GUESTS WILL BE WEAK AT THE KNEES WHEN THEY TASTE THIS MAGICAL MUSSEL COMBINATION.

---

12 mussels on the half shell
¼ cup corn kernels
2 Tbsp chopped fresh mint
2 Tbsp chopped fresh coriander
1 tsp olive oil
2 tsp lemon juice
¼ cup red pepper pesto

1. Remove the mussels from their shells. Reserve the shells.
2. Place the mussels in a pot of simmering water for about 5 minutes. Remove, drain and set aside.
3. In a pan, dry-fry the corn kernels until just charred. Remove and set aside.
4. Combine the mint, coriander, olive oil and lemon juice and pour the mixture over the corn kernels.
5. Place 1 teaspoon of red pepper pesto into the base of each mussel shell.
6. Top each with a mussel and a spoon of the corn salsa and serve.

OYSTERS ON LEEKS

SCIENTISTS BELIEVE THAT THESE LITTLE CRUSTACEANS HAVE BEEN AROUND SINCE THE DINOSAURS AND HAVE BEEN EATEN BY HUMANS FOR EONS. BUT NOWADAYS, WHEN WE THINK OF OYSTERS, WE TYPICALLY THINK OF THEM IN THEIR SHELLS ON A BED OF CRUSHED ICE, SERVED WITH A TOUCH OF LEMON JUICE AND A DASH OF HOT SAUCE. BUT SERVING THE OYSTERS NESTLED IN A CREAMY LEEK SAUCE ADDS A DECADENT TOUCH TO AN ALREADY CLASSY DISH. IT ALSO MAKES IT MORE PALATABLE FOR PEOPLE WHO FIND OYSTERS A LITTLE TOO BRINY. GO ON, TRY ONE — YOU'LL BE COMING BACK FOR MORE.

60g butter
a pinch of sugar
2–3 large leeks, thinly sliced
salt and pepper to taste
2 tsp lemon juice
1 cup dry white wine

½ tsp medium strength curry powder
1 cup cream
2 egg yolks
12 oysters on the half shell
lemon zest for garnishing

1. Melt the butter in a pan, add the sugar and sliced leeks and season with salt and pepper. Cover the pan and slowly cook the leeks until softened. Stir in the lemon juice. Set aside.
2. To a separate pot, add the wine and curry powder, bring to a simmer and cook until the wine has reduced by half. Remove from the heat.
3. Beat together the cream and egg yolks and add to the wine and curry liquid. Reduce the heat and place the pot back on the stove. Stir the mixture until it starts to thicken. Do not let it boil.
4. Season with salt and pepper and stir in the sliced leeks, ensuring that the leeks are well coated.
5. Remove the oysters from their half shell, place a spoonful of the creamy leek mixture into each shell and replace the oyster. Spoon any leftover sauce over the oysters.
6. Arrange the oysters on a baking sheet and place under a grill, just until the oysters are heated through.
7. Garnish with lemon zest and serve.

PRAWN & MUSHROOM PINTXOS

PRAWNS AND SEAFOOD IN GENERAL ARE A DAILY FEATURE ON SPANISH TABLES. THIS IS UNDERSTANDABLE WHEN YOU CONSIDER SPAIN IS SURROUNDED ON THREE SIDES BY WATER. HAVING PRAWNS ON A BAGUETTE IS A QUINTESSENTIAL PINTXOS DISH AND PAIRED HERE WITH MEATY MUSHROOMS, YOU HAVE A DELECTABLE SNACK THAT WILL DISAPPEAR IN A FLASH. BEST OF ALL, PRAWNS ARE HEALTHY TOO, LOADED WITH B VITAMINS AND MINERALS, ARE HIGH IN PROTEIN AND SURPRISINGLY LOW IN CALORIES. SO, FEEL FREE TO TAKE ANOTHER, AND ANOTHER.

4 tsp honey
8 tsp orange juice
4 tsp white wine vinegar
8 tsp olive oil
16 prawns, deveined and shelled
oil for frying

16 slices French baguette
16 button mushrooms, stems removed
4 Tbsp chopped fresh parsley
1 tsp finely chopped garlic
salt and pepper to taste

1. Combine the honey, orange juice, vinegar and 4 teaspoons of the olive oil.
2. Add the prawns to the marinade and set aside.
3. Drizzle a touch of olive oil in a pan and lightly fry the baguette slices on both sides. Remove and set aside.
4. Drizzle a little more olive oil into the same pan, add the mushrooms, stem side down, and cook until golden. Turn the mushrooms over and cook the other side until golden.
5. Combine the parsley, garlic and 4 teaspoons of olive oil and set aside.
6. Pour the prawns, along with the marinade, into the same pan. Season with salt and pepper and cook until done, being careful not to overcook them.
7. Place a mushroom on each slice of baguette, drizzle a little of the parsley and garlic sauce into the centre of each mushroom and finally place a prawn on top.

CHICKEN

Chicken is one of the most popular foods in the world, enjoyed in just about every country – and with good reason. It is readily available just about anywhere and because of its well-earned reputation as a good source of protein and its mild taste and uniform texture, chicken presents a nutritious and intriguing blank canvas with which to get creative. Personally, my favourite thing about cooking with chicken is that it appeals to many different tastes and is flexible enough to fit the flavour palette of almost any cuisine. Chicken has the ability to cross many cultural boundaries with ease and is right at home in this inventive tapas collection.

Chicken has long been considered a staple of a healthy diet. People tend to turn to chicken when they are trying to lose weight or drop their cholesterol because it doesn't have much fat. If you're worried that your chicken tapas will come out dry and boring, then you can relax. These inspired little chicken dishes are packed with flavour and their diverse tapas stylings make each one distinctly delicious from mouthful to mouthful.

This recipe compilation takes chicken from humdrum to super yum and turns out some really special tapas. From tapas chicken wings to Mediterranean chicken pintxos, these delicious and daring chicken-based culinary concepts are designed to be enjoyed to the full.

ARANCINI WITH TRUFFLE DIP

ARANCINI ORIGINATED IN SICILY AROUND THE 10TH CENTURY WHEN THE ISLAND WAS UNDER ARAB RULE, AND THEY'VE BEEN A PART OF ITALIAN CUISINE EVER SINCE. IN EASTERN SICILY, THE BALLS ARE TRADITIONALLY STUFFED WITH A MEAT RAGOUT AND ARE SHAPED MORE CONICALLY, INSPIRED BY MOUNT ETNA. NOWADAYS, THIS ITALIAN FINGER FOOD HAS AS MANY VARIATIONS AS YOU CAN IMAGINE. I'VE COMBINED MY VERSION WITH A TASTY WHITE TRUFFLE DIP.

RISOTTO
¾ cup risotto rice
¼ cup white wine
2½ cups chicken stock
salt and pepper to taste
½ cup grated Parmesan cheese
½ x 250g punnet mushrooms, finely chopped

1 Tbsp olive oil
1 chicken breast, finely chopped
2 tsp sherry vinegar
1 Tbsp plain full cream yoghurt
½ cup cake wheat flour
2 eggs
¾ cup toasted breadcrumbs
cooking oil for frying

Parmesan cheese, finely grated for garnishing
basil leaves for garnishing

TRUFFLE DIP
2 Tbsp mayonnaise
3 Tbsp plain full cream yoghurt
5 tsp white truffle oil

1. The risotto is best if cooked the day before. To cook the risotto, add the risotto rice and white wine to a pot and sauté until the wine has been absorbed.
2. Add some chicken stock and stir continuously until the stock has been absorbed. Continue adding the stock and stirring until all the stock has been absorbed and the risotto is soft. Season with salt and pepper. Stir in the grated Parmesan until the cheese has melted into the risotto.
3. In a separate pan, sauté the mushrooms in the oil until golden brown.
4. Add the chicken breast and sherry vinegar and sauté until the chicken is cooked. Season with salt and pepper and stir in the yoghurt.
5. To make the balls, combine a teaspoon of the risotto and a teaspoon of the mushroom and chicken mixture and roll into a ball, about the size of a golf ball. Continue in this way until you have used up both mixtures.
6. Place the flour into a shallow bowl and the eggs into a separate bowl, whisking the eggs well. Finally, add the breadcrumbs to a third bowl.
7. Dip each ball into the flour, shake off any excess and then roll in the whisked egg. Finally roll each ball in the breadcrumbs, ensuring that it is completely coated.
8. In a pot, heat some oil until hot and fry the balls until golden. You might have to do this in batches. Remove the cooked balls and drain on paper towel.
9. Combine the truffle dip ingredients.
10. Scatter the grated Parmesan cheese and basil leaves over the rice balls and serve with the dip.

TAPAS CHICKEN WINGS

YOU SIMPLY CAN'T TALK ABOUT TAPAS WITHOUT A GOOD CHICKEN WING RECIPE. MARINATED WITH A FIVE-SPICE RUB, GARLIC AND LEMON JUICE, THEY'RE JUICY, TENDER AND TASTY TO BOOT. FIVE-SPICE IS MADE UP OF A BLEND OF CINNAMON, CLOVES, FENNEL, STAR ANISE AND PEPPERCORNS. CINNAMON IS FAMED FOR ITS ANTI-INFLAMMATORY PROPERTIES AND HAS A POWERFUL FLAVOUR THAT BRINGS A LITTLE SOMETHING EXTRA TO THE DISH. THE PERFECT PARTY SNACK, THESE WINGS ARE INTENSELY FLAVOURFUL, AROMATIC AND SO DELICIOUS, THEY'RE PERFECT TO EAT ON THEIR OWN.

1 large onion, chopped
2 Tbsp sweet chilli sauce
¼ cup soy sauce
1 Tbsp finely chopped garlic
1 Tbsp brown sugar
1 Tbsp five-spice powder
600g chicken wings
¼ cup lemon juice
parsley for garnishing
lemon or lime slices for serving

1. Combine the onion, chilli sauce, soy sauce, garlic, sugar and five-spice powder in a bowl.
2. Add the chicken wings and lemon juice and toss well to ensure that the wings are well coated.
3. Cover and refrigerate for at least an hour or preferably overnight.
4. Preheat the oven to 200°C.
5. Remove the chicken wings from the marinade (reserving for dipping later during the cooking process), arrange them on a greased baking sheet and bake in the oven for 10 minutes.
6. Dip each wing in the reserved marinade and place back on the baking sheet.
7. Continue to bake for a further 10 minutes or until the wings are cooked through.
8. Remove and serve scattered with parsley and with lime or lemon slices.

Arancini with truffle dip

Tapas chicken wings

CHICKEN LIVER PÂTÉ WITH CRANBERRY JELLY CUBES

LOVE IT OR HATE IT, CHICKEN LIVER PÂTÉ IS HERE TO STAY. I LIKE TO SERVE MINE WITH THE UNUSUAL ADDITION OF RADIANT CRANBERRY CUBES. THE SWEETNESS OF THE JELLY JUXTAPOSES PERFECTLY WITH THE RICHNESS OF THE PÂTÉ. BEST OF ALL, CHICKEN LIVERS ARE A LOW-COST YET LUXURIOUS ITEM, AND HEALTHWISE THEY'RE RICH IN PROTEIN AND CONTAIN HIGH LEVELS OF MINERALS. WITH THE ADDITION OF CRANBERRIES, THERE'S THE ADDED PUNCH OF EXTRA VITAMIN C. ALL IN ALL, YOU'LL FIND YOUR GUESTS BEGGING FOR YOUR RECIPE.

½ onion, finely chopped
1 tsp olive oil
250g chicken livers
1 slice white bread
2 hard-boiled eggs, chopped
1 Tbsp brandy
salt and pepper to taste
toast of your choice
chopped dried cranberries for garnishing
micro greens for garnishing

CRANBERRY JELLY CUBES
1 Tbsp gelatin
1 cup cranberry juice
1 tsp red wine vinegar
1 Tbsp sugar

1. Fry the onion in the olive oil in a pan until almost softened.
2. Add the chicken livers and sauté until the livers are cooked but still pink in the middle. Remove and place in a bowl.
3. Tear the bread into pieces and add to the livers along with the eggs, brandy, salt and pepper.
4. Using a stick blender, blend all the ingredients until smooth.
5. To make the jelly cubes, sprinkle the gelatin over ¼ cup of the cranberry juice and leave to sponge.
6. Place the balance of the juice into a pot, add the vinegar and sugar and heat until the sugar dissolves, stirring often.
7. Remove from the heat, add the gelatin mixture and stir until combined. Pour the mixture into ice cube trays and place in the fridge to set.
8. Once set, remove the jelly and cut it into 1cm-square cubes.
9. To serve, spread the pâté generously over the toast, add the jelly cubes and scatter over the dried cranberries and micro greens.

CHICKEN PARMIGIANA ON BRINJAL SLICES

THIS RECIPE TURNS CHICKEN PARMIGIANA FROM A CLASSIC MEAL INTO A MOREISH MOUTHFUL. CRISPLY FRIED BRINJALS TOPPED WITH MELTED CHEESE AND CHICKEN AND NESTLED IN A BED OF SAVOURY TOMATO SAUCE ARE GUARANTEED TO KEEP EVERYONE HAPPY. BRINJAL HAS A SPONGY POROUS TEXTURE, WHICH MAKES IT GREAT FOR ABSORBING FLAVOURS. IT'S ALSO FULL OF VITAMINS, MINERALS AND DIETARY FIBRE. MODERN AND ADDICTIVE, THIS IS THE BEST CHICKEN PARM FINGER FOOD AROUND.

125g Emmental cheese, grated
125g Parmesan cheese, grated
4 chicken breast fillets
salt and pepper to taste
16 slices brinjal, about 3mm thick
2 Tbsp olive oil
1 shallot, finely chopped

1 tsp finely chopped garlic
1 Tbsp dried basil
2 tsp dried parsley
2 tsp dried origanum
1 x 400g tin chopped tomatoes
rocket leaves for garnishing

1. Combine the grated Emmental and Parmesan cheeses. Set aside.
2. Cut the chicken breasts in half horizontally to make them thinner.
3. Season both sides with salt and pepper.
4. In a large preheated pan, dry-fry the brinjal slices on both sides until softened. Remove and set aside.
5. In the same pan, heat the olive oil, add the chicken fillets and cook on both sides until just cooked through and golden. Be careful not to overcook the chicken. Remove the chicken, cover to keep warm and set aside.
6. In the same pan, cook the shallot, garlic, the dried herbs and tinned tomatoes for about a minute, stirring to combine all the ingredients.
7. Cut the chicken fillets in half, so that they will fit on the brinjal slices.
8. Arrange the brinjal slices on a greased baking sheet, top with chicken and a spoonful of tomato mixture. Generously scatter over the grated cheese.
9. Place the baking sheet under the grill and grill until the cheese has melted.
10. Garnish with a rocket leaf or two and serve immediately.

MINI SKEWERED CHICKEN WITH A PEANUT COCONUT SAUCE

ALTHOUGH WE ASSOCIATE PEANUT SAUCE WITH INDONESIAN COOKING, PEANUTS WERE ORIGINALLY BROUGHT TO SOUTHEAST ASIA FROM MEXICO VIA PORTUGUESE AND SPANISH MERCHANTS IN THE 1600s. NOWADAYS PEANUT SAUCE IS USED WORLDWIDE AND IS OFTEN MADE WITH PEANUT BUTTER RATHER THAN GROUND PEANUTS. IN KEEPING WITH THE FLAVOURS OF ASIA, I'VE COMBINED THE PEANUT SAUCE WITH COCONUT MILK TO CREATE A DREAMY, CREAMY SAUCE. THE CHICKEN SOAKS UP THE FLAVOURS AND TAKES THIS DISH TO ANOTHER LEVEL. DEFINITELY A CROWD-PLEASER FOR ALL AGES.

2 chicken breast fillets, cut into
   bite-size cubes
½ Tbsp olive oil
cucumber
toothpicks
crushed peanuts and chilli
   flakes to garnish

MARINADE
1 tsp green curry paste
2 Tbsp fish sauce

2 Tbsp soy sauce
1 Tbsp sugar
½ tsp finely chopped ginger
½ tsp finely chopped garlic
1 tsp olive oil

PEANUT COCONUT SAUCE
2 Tbsp finely diced red onion
½ tsp finely chopped ginger
½ tsp chopped garlic
1 tsp sugar

1 Tbsp soy sauce
½ Tbsp fish sauce
¼ tsp red pepper flakes or more
   if you prefer it spicier
½ cup coconut milk
¼ cup smooth peanut butter
½ Tbsp lemon juice

1. Place the chicken cubes and the marinade ingredients in a sealable bag. Seal the bag and gently massage the marinade into the chicken cubes. Set aside for about an hour or longer if possible.
2. While the chicken is marinating, make the peanut sauce by adding the red onion, ginger, garlic, sugar, soy sauce, fish sauce and red pepper flakes to a pot and sautéing gently for 2–3 minutes.
3. Stir in the coconut milk and peanut butter. Cook for a further few minutes, allowing the sauce to thicken somewhat. Stir in the lemon juice and mix well. Remove the pot from the heat and set aside.
4. Heat the oil in a pan and sauté the chicken cubes until just cooked. Be careful not to overcook the chicken.
5. Cut the cucumber in thickish slices so that they're substantial enough to hold, skewer a piece of chicken onto a cucumber slice and scatter over the peanuts and chilli flakes. Serve with the peanut coconut sauce.

CURRIED CHICKEN MINI PITAS WITH MANGO MAYO

THESE PERFECT LITTLE PITA POCKETS ARE STUFFED WITH LIGHTLY CURRIED CHICKEN AND ARE FINISHED OFF WITH A MELLOW MANGO MAYONNAISE AND ROASTED ALMONDS. I LOVE ADDING NUTS TO RECIPES AND ALMONDS ARE A WONDERFUL CHOICE BECAUSE THEY'RE HIGH IN ANTIOXIDANTS THAT CAN PROTECT YOUR CELLS FROM OXIDATIVE DAMAGE, KEEPING YOU LOOKING YOUNGER FOR LONGER. THE FLAVOUR IN THESE CHICKEN PITAS IS BOOSTED BY AN AROMATIC CURRY MARINADE AND A HINT OF CHILLI, AND THEY'RE AS BEAUTIFUL AS THEY ARE DELICIOUS.

2 chicken breast fillets
salt and pepper to taste
10 mini pitas
2 cups finely chopped baby spinach
toasted flaked almonds for garnishing

CURRY MARINADE
¾ tsp finely chopped garlic
¾ tsp finely chopped ginger
½ red onion, finely diced
1 small lemongrass stalk

1 Tbsp lemon juice
½ tsp ground turmeric
½ tsp garam masala
¼ cup coconut cream
¼ cup plain full cream yoghurt
1 chilli, finely diced, or more if you like it spicier
2 Tbsp chopped fresh coriander

MANGO MAYO
½ cup finely diced mango
¾ cup mayonnaise
salt and pepper to taste

1. Place the marinade ingredients in a blender and process until smooth.
2. Slice the chicken fillets in half horizontally to make them thinner.
3. Place the chicken fillets in a bowl and pour over the marinade. Season generously with salt and pepper and stir to ensure that the chicken is well coated.
4. Cover and refrigerate for at least an hour or preferably overnight.
5. In a pan, sauté the chicken until just done. Be careful not to overcook it.
6. Remove the chicken from the pan, shred it finely and set aside.
7. Heat the pitas according to the packet instructions.
8. To make the mango mayo, combine the mango and mayonnaise and season with salt and pepper.
9. Combine the mayo and chicken.
10. To serve, cut the pitas in half, place a spoonful of the chicken mayo mixture into each pita pocket, followed by a spoonful of spinach. Scatter over the flaked almonds and serve.

MEDITERRANEAN CHICKEN PINTXOS

THESE PINTXOS ABOUND WITH MEDITERRANEAN FLAVOURS. WHETHER IT'S THE SOFTER TASTING SHERRY VINEGAR OR THE INTENSITY OF THE SUNDRIED TOMATOES, THEY ARE SIMPLY BURSTING WITH ALL THAT IS GOOD ABOUT THE MED. THEY ARE BRIMMING WITH VEGGIES FROM GREEN PEPPER TO BRINJAL, SO THEY ARE HEALTHY TOO AND MAKE AN EXCELLENT LIGHTER OPTION FOR A LEISURELY LUNCH WITH FRIENDS.

2 brinjals, sliced about 5mm thick
2 Tbsp olive oil
5–7 deboned chicken thighs, cut into strips
3 cups sliced mushrooms
1 green pepper, chopped
1 tsp dried origanum
2 Tbsp sherry vinegar
2 tsp lemon juice
½ tsp finely chopped garlic
1 Tbsp salted butter
salt and pepper to taste

10–12 slices French baguette
10–12 baby spinach leaves
10–12 sundried tomatoes, halved for garnishing
Parmesan cheese shavings for garnishing

PICKLED ASPARAGUS
1 Tbsp sugar
1 Tbsp white wine vinegar
2 Tbsp water
3 large asparagus, shaved (use a potato peeler)

WHOLEGRAIN MUSTARD SAUCE
¼ cup wholegrain mustard
¼ cup sour cream
⅓ cup plain full cream yoghurt
2 Tbsp olive oil

1. To make the pickled asparagus, combine the sugar, vinegar and water. Add the shaved asparagus and leave to pickle for about half an hour.
2. In a heated pan, dry-fry the brinjal slices until browned. Turn and brown the other side, then remove and set aside.
3. In the same pan, add 1 tablespoon of the olive oil and, on a high heat, fry the chicken strips until browned.
4. Lower the heat, add the mushrooms, green pepper, origanum, sherry vinegar, lemon juice, garlic and butter and sauté until the mushrooms are browned and the chicken is just cooked. Season with salt and pepper.
5. Combine the wholegrain mustard sauce ingredients and set aside.
6. To serve, lightly toast the baguette slices. Spread some mustard sauce on each slice, add a slice of brinjal, a leaf or two of baby spinach, followed by the chicken mixture. Add 2 pieces of sundried tomatoes and finally scatter over the pickled asparagus and shaved Parmesan cheese.

DECONSTRUCTED CHICKEN CORDON BLEU

IF YOU'RE A CHICKEN CORDON BLEU LOVER, I GUARANTEE YOU'RE GOING TO LOVE THIS DECONSTRUCTED VERSION. IT'S ALSO MUCH EASIER TO MAKE THAN THE TRADITIONAL VERSION, WHILE STILL KEEPING EVERYTHING THAT WE LOVE ABOUT THE FRENCH DISH. CHICKEN IS ONE OF THE MOST COMMONLY FOUND FOODS AROUND THE WORLD, BUT COMMON DOESN'T MEAN UNHEALTHY. EATING CHICKEN BREAST SUPPRESSES AND CONTROLS A BODY'S HOMOCYSTEINE AMINO ACID LEVELS WHICH, IF TOO HIGH, CAN LEAD TO CARDIOVASCULAR DISEASE, SO IT'S GREAT HEART-SMART FOOD.

12 wooden skewers
3 uncooked chicken schnitzels, store bought
4–5 slices ham
12 cubes Emmental cheese, about 1cm square
fresh thyme for garnishing

CHEESE & MUSTARD SAUCE
2 Tbsp butter
2 Tbsp cake wheat flour
1 cup milk
2 Tbsp Dijon mustard
¼ cup grated Parmesan cheese
salt and pepper to taste

1. Preheat the oven to 200°C.
2. Soak the skewers in water for at least half an hour to stop them from burning.
3. Cook the chicken schnitzels according to the packet instructions. Once cool enough to handle, cut into bite-size pieces.
4. Slice the ham into strips and wrap them around the cheese cubes.
5. To make the sauce, melt the butter in a pot and add the flour, stirring constantly.
6. Pour in the milk slowly and continue to stir.
7. Add the mustard, Parmesan cheese and season generously with salt and pepper. Continue stirring until the cheese has melted. Set aside.
8. Onto each skewer, thread one piece of chicken followed by the ham-wrapped cheese and another piece of chicken.
9. Place the skewers on a greased baking sheet and grill for about 2 minutes, turn and continue to grill until the cheese is just starting to melt.
10. Remove to a serving platter and allow to cool slightly before pouring over the cheese and mustard sauce. Scatter over some fresh thyme and serve.

Mediterranean chicken pintxos

**Deconstructed chicken
cordon bleu**

GREEN TEA CHICKEN PINTXOS

LOOKING FOR A CHICKEN RECIPE THAT REALLY STANDS OUT? YOU'VE FOUND IT! THIS TENDER CHICKEN IS COVERED WITH A DELECTABLE ASIAN-INSPIRED GREEN TEA SPICE. GREEN TEA HAS SO MANY HEALTH BENEFITS. IT'S GREAT FOR INCREASING METABOLISM, PROMOTING HEALTHY GUMS AND IT TASTES AMAZING WHEN COMBINED WITH THE EARTHY FLAVOURS OF THE BEETROOT AND THE SALTINESS OF THE FETA. IT LOOKS FANCY, BUT IT'S DECEPTIVELY SIMPLE. PERFECT FOR YOUR TAPAS TABLE.

2 chicken breast fillets
2 bags green tea, lemon flavour
salt and pepper to taste
1–2 Tbsp olive oil
12–14 slices French baguette
12–14 rocket leaves
2–3 Tbsp toasted pine nuts
¼ cup crumbled feta
2–3 pickled beetroot, sliced for garnishing

BEETROOT HUMMUS

1 x 400g tin chickpeas, drained
   and liquid reserved
6 Tbsp reserved chickpea liquid
2 beetroots, peeled and cooked
5 Tbsp lemon juice
2 Tbsp tahini
2 cloves garlic, crushed
½ tsp salt
4 Tbsp olive oil
1 tsp ground cumin

1. Cut the chicken breasts in half horizontally, then slice into strips.
2. Empty the green tea bags into a shallow bowl and add salt and pepper.
3. Roll the chicken pieces in the tea seasoning, ensuring that the chicken is well coated.
4. In a pan, heat the olive oil until hot and add the chicken pieces.
5. Sauté the chicken pieces until they're browned and just cooked. Be careful not to overcook the chicken. Remove and keep warm.
6. To make the beetroot hummus, whizz the chickpeas in a blender and then add the remaining hummus ingredients. Blend to a smooth paste, then season to taste.
7. To serve, spread the baguette slices generously with the beetroot hummus, add a leaf or two of rocket and a couple of pieces of chicken. Scatter over the pine nuts and crumbled feta and finish off with a slice of beetroot.

SWEET CHILLI CHICKEN BALLS ON NACHOS

TRY THIS NEW TAKE ON AN OLD FAVOURITE. ONE NORMALLY ASSOCIATES NACHOS CHIPS WITH LOADS OF GOOEY MELTED CHEESE BUT HERE THEY'RE LOADED WITH HEALTHY, CREAMY AND OH SO DELICIOUS MASHED AVOCADO. NACHOS CHIPS ARE THE PERFECT SHAPE FOR THESE TAPAS AS THEY MAKE A SURPRISING HOLDER FOR THE SOFT, JUICY CHICKEN BALLS, WHICH ARE IN PERFECT CONTRAST TO THE CRUNCHINESS OF THE NACHOS. NESTLED ON SOME HEALTHY AVO, ROUNDED OFF WITH SOME SWEET CHILLI SAUCE AND YOU HAVE A FUN MEXICAN-STYLED SNACK THAT YOU CAN ENJOY WITH A MARGARITA OR THREE.

MAKES ABOUT 20 CHICKEN BALLS

CHICKEN BALLS
½ onion, chopped
5 capers
2 slices day-old bread,
    crusts removed
250–300g chicken mince
1 egg

1½ Tbsp tomato sauce
1 Tbsp Worcestershire sauce
1½ tsp dried origanum
¼ tsp finely chopped garlic
salt and pepper to taste
olive oil for frying
toothpicks to serve

1–2 avocados, mashed
salt and pepper to taste
splash of lemon juice
20 nachos chips or similar
sweet chilli sauce for drizzling
10 small cherry tomatoes,
    halved

1. To make the chicken balls, whizz the onion, capers and slices of bread in a blender or food processer until well combined.
2. Mix in the chicken and egg. Add the tomato sauce, Worcestershire sauce, origanum, garlic, salt and pepper and mix until well combined.
3. Roll the mixture into 2.5cm–3cm little balls and refrigerate for 30–60 minutes.
4. Heat the olive oil in a pan and fry the balls until cooked and golden. Drain on paper towel.
5. Mash the avocado, season with salt and pepper and stir in a splash of lemon juice to stop the avocado from turning brown.
6. To assemble, place a dollop of mashed avocado onto each nachos chip and season.
7. Place a chicken ball on top of the avocado and drizzle over some sweet chilli sauce. Secure a halved cherry tomato to each chicken ball with a toothpick.
8. An alternative serving suggestion is to use individual dessertspoons: place 1 or 2 teaspoons of avocado into the base of the spoon, place a chicken ball on top, drizzle over a little sweet chilli sauce and skewer with a halved cherry tomato. Finally place a nachos chip at an angle into the avocado.

CHICKEN BLUE CHEESE BITES

IF YOU NEED A TAPAS THAT EVERYONE AT THE PARTY WILL BE SURE TO LOVE, THEN THESE BEAUTIFUL CHICKEN BITES ARE HERE TO LEVEL UP YOUR SNACK GAME. SAUTÉED AND SKEWERED WITH MUSHROOMS AND SPINACH LEAVES AND SERVED WITH A BLUE CHEESE DIP THAT BRINGS ALL THE FLAVOURS TOGETHER, YOU MIGHT GO THROUGH HALF A TRAY BEFORE THE PARTY EVEN STARTS. BLUE CHEESE IS ALSO VERY NUTRITIOUS AND BOASTS MORE CALCIUM THAN OTHER CHEESES, SO LOOKING AFTER YOUR BONE HEALTH IS THE PERFECT EXCUSE TO INDULGE IN THESE DELICIOUS DIPPERS.

2 chicken breast fillets
1 Tbsp olive oil
½ tsp dried mixed herbs
salt and pepper to taste
½ tsp dried basil
1 Tbsp breadcrumbs
6 portabella mushrooms, halved
12 baby spinach leaves
12 small skewers

BLUE CHEESE DIP
50g blue cheese
1 Tbsp cream
2 Tbsp plain full cream yoghurt
½ tsp dried rosemary

1. Slice the chicken breast fillets into bite-size pieces.
2. Heat the oil in a pan, add the chicken and sauté until just browned.
3. Sprinkle over the mixed herbs, salt and pepper, basil and breadcrumbs and stir together, coating the chicken strips.
4. Continue to cook until the chicken is done. Be careful not to overcook it. Remove the chicken and keep warm.
5. In the same pan, sauté the mushrooms until they are softened and browned.
6. In a separate small pot over a low heat, combine the dip ingredients, stirring gently until the blue cheese melts.
7. To serve, wrap a piece of chicken in a spinach leaf, spear onto a skewer together with half a mushroom and serve with the cheese dip.

GRANADILLA CHICKEN ON POTATO SLICES

THIS RECIPE IS AS GORGEOUS AS IT IS TASTY: CHICKEN PIECES STACKED ON WHOLESOME POTATO SLICES AND FINISHED WITH A DAZZLING GRANADILLA SAUCE. THE FLAVOURS OF GINGER AND GRANADILLA MAKE A SWEET-SAVOURY SAUCE FOR TENDER CHICKEN IN THIS UNUSUAL AND TASTY RECIPE. GRANADILLAS ARE A GOOD SOURCE OF FIBRE, VITAMINS C AND A AND, SINCE THEY ARE HIGH IN NUTRIENTS BUT LOW IN CALORIES, YOU CAN ADD THEM TO YOUR DIET WITH EASE. THIS RECIPE IS CREATIVE WHILE STILL STAYING TOTALLY SCRUMPTIOUS, A DEFINITE WIN FOR ANY OCCASION.

8–10 baby potatoes, unpeeled, cooked, topped and tailed
4–5 deboned chicken thighs
olive oil for frying
2 cups chicken stock
4 granadillas
4 tsp finely chopped ginger
2 Tbsp brown sugar
2 Tbsp white wine vinegar
2 Tbsp soy sauce
2 Tbsp cornflour
4 spring onions, sliced on the diagonal
handful of baby spinach, finely sliced

1. Slice the potatoes about 1cm thick and set aside.
2. Chop the chicken thighs into bite-size pieces and sauté in a pan with a touch of olive oil until just browned. Remove the chicken and set aside.
3. In the same pan, combine the chicken stock, granadilla pulp, ginger, sugar, vinegar and soy sauce and simmer for a few minutes.
4. Mix the cornflour with a little water to form a paste and stir it into the granadilla sauce until the sauce thickens.
5. Stir in the chicken pieces, ensuring that they're well coated and just cooked.
6. To serve, place a piece or two of chicken onto each potato slice, spoon any extra sauce over and then scatter over the spring onions and baby spinach.

MEAT

Every event, big or small, stands to benefit from the addition of an assortment of mouthwatering meaty tapas. While vegetarianism is on the rise, there's still a huge contingent of meat eaters to be catered for. The carnivores in your life will certainly be happy when you serve up these full-flavoured meat bites at your next gathering.

Whether you're an aspiring home cook attempting tapas for the first time or a more experienced cook looking to expand your repertoire, then these hearty and wholesome delights are sure to satisfy your guests – no matter the occasion. In this recipe selection you'll find a variety of tapas that are easy to prepare in any kitchen, yet so tasty that your guests will think you slaved over them for hours. So how about replacing your usual fare with exotic game dishes like ostrich and raspberry chutney, or stay with the Spanish theme and serve the decadent beef and caprese pintxos or, to keep it more South African, the bobotie cups?

By using interesting ingredients and unusual ways of plating, you can wow your guests with meaty party platters that are a feast for the eyes and the mouth. Whatever you choose from this collection, you're guaranteed tender, tasty, meaty tapas to enjoy with friends and family and with a jug or two of sangria.

SPICY PORK MINI TACOS

MINI TACOS ARE THE PERFECT INCLUSION ON A TAPAS TABLE. NOT QUITE A PINTXOS BUT DEFINITELY IN KEEPING WITH THE THEME. TOPPED OFF WITH ALL THE MEXICAN GOODNESS THAT YOU'VE COME TO EXPECT FROM TACOS BUT WITH AN UNEXPECTED FUSION OF ASIAN FLAVOURS, THESE LIGHTLY SPICED PORK TACOS ARE FUN TO MAKE AND CAN BE READY IN A FLASH, JUST THE THING FOR AN EASY FLAVOURSOME TREAT.

2 tsp finely chopped ginger
2 tsp finely chopped garlic
1 Tbsp finely chopped red chilli
½ cup soy sauce
½ cup orange juice
6–8 pork loin chops
oil for sautéing
1 red onion, finely diced
1 x 410g tin whole kernel corn, drained

salt and pepper to taste
chilli flakes (optional)
¼ cup lemon juice
16 small corn taco shells
2 avocados, peeled and chopped
2 cups shredded lettuce
½ cup chopped fresh coriander
1 cup sour cream

1. Combine the ginger, garlic, chilli, soy sauce and orange juice.
2. Cut the pork meat off the bone, dice into bite-size pieces and add to the sauce.
3. Place in the fridge and let the pork rest in the marinade for at least half an hour.
4. Heat some oil in a pan, then add the onion, corn, pork with the marinade sauce and salt and pepper and sauté until the pork is cooked. Sprinkle over the chilli flakes if using.
5. Stir in 2–3 tablespoons of the lemon juice.
6. Heat the taco shells according to the packet instructions.
7. Pour the balance of the lemon juice over the chopped avocado to stop it from going brown.
8. To assemble, combine the lettuce and coriander and place in the taco shells. Add the pork, avocado and a generous dollop of sour cream and serve immediately.

MOROCCAN LAMB TAPAS

TENDER LAMB COATED IN A HEADY MIX OF MOROCCAN SPICES, NESTLED ON A BRIGHT GREEN PEA PURÉE, IS INTOXICATING. THE MEDLEY OF FLAVOURS IN THIS RECIPE LENDS A REFRESHING COOLNESS TO THE DISH THAT BALANCES OUT THE SPICE PERFECTLY. WHEN THE FAT HAS BEEN TRIMMED, LAMB CAN BE AN EXCELLENT CHOICE FOR A HEALTHY DIET SINCE IT'S SO RICH IN HIGH-QUALITY PROTEIN, VITAMINS AND MINERALS. WITH AN INVIGORATING BLEND OF SPICES AND AN INTRICATE SWEET AND SAVOURY FLAVOUR PROFILE, THIS IS A BEAUTIFULLY TEXTURED DISH THAT YOU'LL MAKE MORE THAN ONCE.

550g lamb loin chops, bones and fat removed
vegetable oil for frying
plain full cream yoghurt for garnishing
micro herbs for garnishing
edible flowers to garnish (optional)

MOROCCAN SPICE
1 tsp ground cumin
1 tsp ground coriander
1 tsp ground ginger
½ tsp ground cinnamon
½ tsp cayenne pepper
salt and pepper to taste

PEA PURÉE
¼ tsp finely chopped garlic
1 tsp olive oil
½ cup vegetable stock
250g frozen baby peas
2 Tbsp lemon juice
salt and pepper to taste
2 Tbsp plain full cream yoghurt
2½ Tbsp finely chopped fresh mint

1. Cut the lamb into bite-size pieces.
2. To make the Moroccan spice, combine the spice ingredients in a bowl. Toss the lamb pieces in the spice mix, coating well.
3. In a preheated pan, heat 1 tablespoon of vegetable oil and quickly sauté the lamb pieces, ensuring that they're seared but not overcooked.
4. Remove and allow to rest while you make the pea purée.
5. In a small pan, sauté the garlic in the olive oil. Once softened, add the vegetable stock, frozen peas and lemon juice and simmer for 3–4 minutes until the peas have softened.
6. Remove from the heat, season with salt and pepper, set aside to cool.
7. Place the pea mixture in a blender together with the yoghurt and mint and blend until smooth.
8. To serve, add a dollop of the pea purée to individual bowls and place a piece or two of the lamb on top. Garnish with a dollop of yoghurt, scatter over some micro herbs and serve.

BEEF LOLLIPOP PIES

DITCH THE KNIFE AND FORK! YOU DON'T NEED THEM WHEN YOU BITE INTO THESE TASTY PIES ON A STICK. THESE FUN AND FUNKY LOLLIPOP PIES TAKE TRADITIONAL BEEF PIES FROM TEDIOUS TO TERRIFIC. THEY'RE EASY AND FUN TO MAKE AND ARE STUFFED WITH SAUCY SIRLOIN STEAK. NOW, SIRLOIN MIGHT NOT BE THE FIRST FOOD THAT COMES TO MIND WHEN PUTTING TOGETHER A PIE, BUT IT IS AN EXCELLENT SOURCE OF HIGH-QUALITY PROTEIN AND ESSENTIAL AMINO ACIDS. THESE PIES ARE A CINCH TO MAKE AND SERVE TO CARNIVORES AND, BEST OF ALL, THEY MAKE A GREAT DISPLAY TOO.

12 lollipop sticks
½ onion, finely chopped
400g sirloin steak, fat removed, and cubed
1 x 200g packet streaky bacon, finely chopped
12 mushrooms, finely chopped
2 carrots, finely chopped
2 Tbsp olive oil
1 tsp finely chopped garlic
1 tsp dried thyme
1 Tbsp tomato paste

2 beef stock cubes
2½ cups red wine
1½ cups water
salt and pepper to taste
1 x 400g packet ready rolled puff pastry
whisked egg for brushing
2 Tbsp poppy seeds
chutney to serve (optional)

1. Soak the lollipop sticks in cold water for about half an hour so that they don't burn when placed in the oven.
2. Gently sauté the onion, steak, bacon, mushrooms and carrots in the oil in a pot until they start to soften.
3. Stir in the garlic, thyme, tomato paste, stock cubes, red wine and ½ cup of the water. Season with salt and pepper.
4. Gently simmer for about 30 minutes. If the mixture becomes dry, add another ½ cup of water.
5. Preheat the oven to 170°C.
6. Roll out the puff pastry and cut out 24 circles using a 7cm cookie cutter.
7. Place a lollipop stick onto half of the circles.
8. Place 1–2 teaspoons of the meat mixture into the centre of the circles with sticks.
9. Place the balance of the pastry circles on top of the meat mixture, and, using a fork, seal all around, making especially sure that the pastry is well sealed around the lollipop stick.
10. Place the lollipop pies on a greased baking sheet, brush with the whisked egg and scatter over the poppy seeds. Prick the pastry with a fork and bake in the oven for about 20 minutes or until the puff pastry has turned golden.
11. Remove and serve with chutney (optional).

BOBOTIE CUPS

IT'S ALLEGED THAT THE FIRST BOBOTIE RECIPE APPEARED IN A DUTCH COOKBOOK IN 1609 AND WAS BROUGHT TO SOUTH AFRICA BY THE DUTCH SETTLERS WHERE IT WAS EMBRACED BY THE CAPE MALAYS. BUT BY WHATEVER MEANS IT GOT HERE, WE SOUTH AFRICANS HAVE MADE IT OUR OWN. IN THIS RECIPE, THE CLASSIC DISH IS GIVEN A MINOR MAKEOVER BY BEING SERVED IN INDIVIDUAL RICE CUPS. BUT NONE OF THAT HEARTY AND COMFORTING FLAVOUR IS COMPROMISED. BEST OF ALL, THE EGG CUSTARD IS STILL A FEATURE, GARNISHED WITH SOME BANANA SLICES IF YOU LIKE.

2 Tbsp olive oil
2 tsp finely chopped garlic
1 onion, chopped
2 tsp finely chopped ginger
1 tsp curry powder
1 tsp ground turmeric
1 tsp ground cumin
1 tsp ground coriander
1 tsp ground cinnamon
500g lean beef mince
1 slice white bread

1 bay leaf
2 Tbsp water
2 Tbsp Worcestershire sauce
2 Tbsp tomato paste
3–4 Tbsp chutney
2 Tbsp lemon juice
½ apple, grated
salt and pepper to taste
plain yoghurt for serving
chopped banana for garnishing

RICE CUPS
2 eggs
1 cup cooked basmati rice
salt and pepper to taste

CUSTARD TOPPING
1 cup milk
2 eggs
2 Tbsp butter, melted
salt and pepper to taste

1. In a large pot, heat the oil and sauté the garlic, onion and ginger until the onion has softened.
2. Add the spices and stir for a minute.
3. Add the mince and continue to cook until the mince has browned. Stir often so that there aren't any lumps.
4. Add the remaining ingredients, except the yoghurt and banana, and continue to simmer for about 20 minutes. Remove the pot from the heat, take out the bay leaf and set aside.
5. Preheat the oven to 180°C.
6. To make the rice cups, combine the eggs, cooked basmati rice and salt and pepper.
7. Using a greased muffin tin, place a spoonful or two of rice mixture into each muffin hole and press it down and up the sides, covering most of the muffin hole.
8. Place in the oven and bake for about 20 minutes or until the rice is golden and set.
9. Remove the muffin tin and add a spoonful or two of meat mixture to each rice cup.
10. Combine the custard topping ingredients, seasoning generously with salt and pepper, and pour a small amount over the meat.
11. Bake in the oven for 7–10 minutes or until the custard has set.
12. Remove the muffin tin and once cool enough to handle, remove the bobotie cups and serve with a dollop of plain yoghurt and a garnish of chopped banana.

SPICY KEEMA CUPS

I LOVE THE CONCEPT OF EDIBLE CUPS. IT'S THE FOOD THAT SERVES ITSELF! THESE KEEMA CURRY CUPS ARE MADE UP OF INCREDIBLY FLAVOURFUL GROUND BEEF CURRY WITH PEAS – THE VERY DEFINITION OF COMFORT FOOD – ALL IN AN EASY-TO-EAT CONTAINER. YOUR GUESTS WILL DEFINITELY BE IMPRESSED WITH THESE CLEVER LITTLE CUPS, AND THE BEST PART, NO BOWLS TO WASH UP AFTERWARDS.

IF IT WEREN'T FOR INDIA, OUR FOOD WOULD MOST LIKELY TASTE A WHOLE LOT BLANDER AND WE WOULDN'T BE ABLE TO ENJOY THE AMAZING HEALTH BENEFITS THAT COME WITH GARAM MASALA. APART FROM BOOSTING DIGESTION, IT ALSO HELPS WITH NAUSEA.

1 tsp olive oil
500g beef mince
1 red onion, finely diced
1 tsp finely chopped garlic
1 tsp finely chopped ginger
1 tsp ground cumin
2 tsp garam masala
1 tsp ground coriander
1 tsp medium strength curry
   powder

½ tsp ground turmeric
2 tsp tomato paste
½ cup water
½ cup baby peas
salt and pepper to taste
3 wholewheat wraps
melted butter for brushing
fresh coriander for garnishing
chopped chillies for
   garnishing

RAITA
5cm piece English cucumber
2 tsp lemon juice
¼ cup plain full cream yoghurt
salt and pepper to taste

1. Preheat the oven to 180°C.
2. Heat the oil in a pan and sauté the mince until it starts to brown.
3. Add the onion and continue to cook until the meat is completely brown and cooked through.
4. Stir in the spices and tomato paste and continue to cook for another minute or two. Pour in the water, add the peas and continue to sauté until the water has evaporated. Season with salt and pepper.
5. To make the raita, grate the cucumber with the skin on and combine with the lemon juice and yoghurt. Season with salt and pepper.
6. Using a cookie cutter, cut out 10cm circles from the wraps. Brush both sides lightly with melted butter.
7. Place the wrap circles into the cups of a muffin tin and bake for 5–10 minutes or until they are browned.
8. Remove the cups from the oven and fill with the mince mixture. Top each one with raita, sprigs of coriander and chopped chillies.

Bobotie cups

Spicy keema cups

RASPBERRY CHUTNEY OSTRICH SLICES

OSTRICH IS A WONDERFUL MEAT TO COOK: IT TASTES LIKE BEEF FILLET BUT HAS A MUCH LOWER FAT CONTENT, AND THE LITTLE FAT THAT IT DOES CONTAIN IS UNSATURATED, MEANING IT'S REALLY GOOD FOR YOU. THIS RECIPE MAKES THE MOST OF THAT LEANNESS BY ADDING A RADIANT RASPBERRY CHUTNEY INTO THE MIX.

3–4 ostrich medallions
salt and pepper to taste
oil for sautéing
1–2 Tbsp balsamic vinegar
1–2 Tbsp Worcestershire sauce
2 large potatoes, unpeeled
2 tsp olive oil
mascarpone cheese for
    garnishing

roasted pine nuts for
    garnishing
¼ cup shaved Parmesan
    cheese
¼ cup shredded rocket
wooden skewers to serve
    (optional)

BERRY CHUTNEY
1½ tsp olive oil

1 shallot, finely chopped
2 Tbsp chopped dried
    cranberries
½ cup raspberries
2 tsp orange marmalade
2 Tbsp red wine vinegar
½ tsp finely chopped ginger
¼ tsp allspice
1 Tbsp sugar
½ tsp lemon juice

1. To make the chutney, add the olive oil and chopped shallot to a pot and sweat gently until the shallot has softened.
2. Add the remaining ingredients and continue to simmer until the chutney has thickened, 20–30 minutes. Remove the pot from the heat and set aside.
3. Season the ostrich medallions generously with salt and pepper.
4. In a pan on high heat, heat a little oil and sear the medallions on both sides. Turn down the heat, pour the vinegar and Worcestershire sauce over the medallions and continue to cook until done to your liking. I prefer it quite pink as ostrich gets very tough the longer you cook it. Once cooked to your preference, remove the medallions, cover and keep warm and allow to rest for at least 10 minutes.
5. Boil the potatoes until just done. When cool enough to handle, slice the potatoes thickly and fry them in the olive oil until golden on both sides.
6. To serve, slice the medallions thickly, place a spoonful of berry chutney on top of a potato slice and add a slice or two of ostrich.
7. Add a dollop of mascarpone, scatter over some pine nuts along with some shaved Parmesan and finish off with some shredded rocket.
8. Use skewers to hold the ingredients together, if necessary.

ARTICHOKE &
PARMA HAM SKEWERS

ARTICHOKES ARE AN UNDERRATED FOOD AND FRANKLY THEY'RE A MYSTERY TO MOST PEOPLE. THEY ARE LOW IN FAT, HIGH IN FIBRE AND LOADED WITH VITAMINS C AND K, FOLATE, PHOSPHORUS AND MAGNESIUM. THEY'RE HEALTHY, HEARTY AND WHOLESOME, AND WHEN MARINATED AND SKEWERED WITH SULTRY, SALTY PARMA HAM, THEY'RE DOWNRIGHT DELICIOUS. COMPLEMENTARY COLOURS, TEXTURES AND TASTES MAKE THIS RECIPE ANOTHER CROWD-PLEASER, TURNING JUST ABOUT ANYONE INTO AN ARTICHOKE ADDICT.

1 x 250g jar grilled artichokes
1 Tbsp olive oil
¼ red onion, finely diced
¼ green pepper, finely diced
½ tsp finely chopped garlic
½ tsp dried thyme
½ tsp dried parsley

125g tomato purée
1 Tbsp basil pesto
100g Parma ham
toothpicks

1. Drain a jar of quartered artichoke hearts and set aside.
2. In a pan, heat the oil and gently sauté the onion, green pepper, garlic and herbs until the onion and pepper have softened.
3. Remove the pan from the heat and allow the mixture to cool slightly.
4. In a blender, combine the cooled mixture, tomato purée and basil pesto and blend until smooth. Pour into a small bowl.
5. Slice the Parma ham in half, lengthways.
6. To serve, roll up each piece of Parma ham, pierce it with a toothpick and then add a quartered artichoke. Serve with the blended sauce.

CUBED PORK BELLY ON APPLE SLICES

PORK BELLY HAS BECOME A FIXTURE ON MANY MENUS OVER THE LAST FEW YEARS AND ITS SUCCESS CAN BE PUT DOWN TO ITS INTENSE UMAMI FLAVOUR AND CRISP CRACKLING. THIS PORK BELLY WITH APPLE RECIPE BRINGS THE BEST OUT OF THE CUT, AS THE APPLES CUT THROUGH THE FATTINESS OF THE PORK. APPLES MAY AID WEIGHT LOSS IN SEVERAL WAYS, AND THEY ARE ALSO PARTICULARLY FILLING DUE TO THEIR HIGH FIBRE CONTENT. WITH ALL THAT PORKY PERFECTION, THESE SLICES OF HEAVEN WILL DEFINITELY BE ADDED TO YOUR FAVOURITES FOLDER.

200–300g pork belly
2 tsp Chinese five-spice powder
¼ cup soy sauce
¼ cup honey
1 tsp fish sauce
1 Tbsp red wine vinegar

salt and pepper to taste
1 apple
lemon juice to stop the apple from browning
about ¼ cup sour cream
chopped chives for garnishing

1. Pat the pork belly dry with paper towel and slice into 4cm lengths.
2. Rub the Chinese five-spice powder on all sides of the belly, except for the skin.
3. In a large pan, dry-sear the belly slices on all sides, except for the skin.
4. Remove and, once cool enough to handle, slice off the skin and set aside.
5. In a flat dish, combine the soy sauce, honey, fish sauce, vinegar, salt and pepper.
6. Cut the pork belly into bite-size pieces and add to the sauce. Mix well, ensuring that the meat is completely coated. Allow to marinate for about 1 hour or longer if possible.
7. While the meat is marinating, place the skin on a greased baking sheet. Generously season the skin with salt and place under the grill for 15–20 minutes or until the skin is crisp. Turn the skin over and crisp the other side. Remove the baking sheet from the oven and, once cool enough to handle, break the crackling into pieces and set aside.
8. Remove the meat from the marinade and, in the same large pan, sauté the pork belly bites until cooked. Halfway through, pour over a touch more marinade, but be careful not to burn the pork. Remove the pan from the heat and set aside.
9. Cut the apple into 3mm-thick slices and about the same size as the pork bites. Sprinkle over some lemon juice to stop the apples from turning brown.
10. To serve, place a piece of pork belly onto a slice of apple, add a dollop of sour cream, scatter over the chopped chives and serve with a piece of crackling.

GOURMET 'HOT DOG' PINTXOS

FORGET ABOUT HAVING HOT DOGS AT THE KIDDIES' TABLE. THESE GOURMET BOCKWURST HOT DOGS TURN UP THE HEAT AND GIVE THE HUMBLE HOT DOG AN ADULT MAKEOVER. A GOOD GOURMET DOG IS ALL ABOUT THE TOPPINGS AND THIS RECIPE HAS THAT IN SPADES. WITH A LIGHTLY SPICED CHILLI MAYO AND GHERKIN RELISH, THESE DOGS WILL HAVE YOU HOWLING FOR MORE. CHILLI PEPPERS ARE RICH IN ANTIOXIDANTS, MOST NOTABLY CAPSAICIN, WHICH IS RESPONSIBLE FOR THE SPICY TASTE OF THE MAYO. A SIMPLE PARTY SNACK NO MORE, IT'S THE GOURMET HOT DOGS' TIME TO SHINE.

---

2 large onions, finely sliced
¼ cup olive oil
¼ cup white wine vinegar
2 Tbsp sugar
2 tsp finely chopped red chilli
4 tsp tangy mayonnaise
4 tsp honey mustard

4 bockwurst sausages
16 slices French baguette
butter for spreading
8 sweet and sour gherkins, sliced lengthways
chopped chives for garnishing

1. In a pan, sauté the onions, olive oil and vinegar over a low heat.
2. After a few minutes, stir in the sugar and continue to simmer for about 10 minutes until the onions have softened and caramelised.
3. Once the onions have caramelised, remove and set aside.
4. In a bowl, combine the red chilli, mayonnaise and honey mustard.
5. In the same pan used to cook the onions, gently fry the bockwurst until just charred.
6. Toast the French bread, spread a touch of butter over each slice, followed by a dab of chilli mayo.
7. Slice the bockwurst thickly on the diagonal and place a slice or two on each slice of toast.
8. Add a slice or two of gherkin and a generous portion of caramelised onions, followed by another dollop of the chilli mayo. Sprinkle over the chopped chives.

BEEF & HORSERADISH PINTXOS

BEEF AND HORSERADISH AREN'T JUST FOR STUFFY SUNDAY LUNCHES ANY MORE. THIS CLASSIC COMBO IS BELOVED BY MANY, AND NOW YOU CAN HAVE IT ANY TIME. HORSERADISH IS A MARVELLOUS CONDIMENT AND EVEN IN SMALL AMOUNTS IT PROVIDES SEVERAL POTENTIAL HEALTH BENEFITS. IT CONTAINS GLYCOSYLATES AND ISOTHIOCYANATES, WHICH FIGHT BACTERIAL AND FUNGAL INFECTIONS, AND IT IMPROVES BREATHING ISSUES. GET READY FOR A TASTE EXPERIENCE YOU WON'T SOON FORGET.

200g rump steak
salt and pepper to taste
1–2 Tbsp hot mustard
1–2 Tbsp vegetable oil for sautéing
2 Tbsp crème fraîche

2 Tbsp creamed horseradish
12 slices French baguette, lightly toasted
½ cup shaved Parmesan cheese
chopped chives for garnishing

1. Generously season both sides of the steak with salt and pepper and spread with hot mustard.
2. Heat a griddle pan and some oil until hot, then grill the steak for a few minutes until there are dark griddle lines, then turn and continue to grill on the other side.
3. Once grilled to your liking (I like it medium rare), remove and set aside to rest for about 10 minutes.
4. While the meat is resting, combine the crème fraîche and creamed horseradish, ensuring that they're well mixed.
5. Cut the steak into thick slices.
6. To assemble, generously spread the horseradish and crème fraiche mixture over each slice of toast, add a slice or two of steak, followed by the Parmesan shavings and a scattering of chopped chives.

COLOURFUL BEEF PINTXOS

I LOVE THE CONTRASTS IN THIS DISH. THERE'S THE HEARTY STEAK, JUXTAPOSED WITH THE FRESHNESS OF THE TOMATOES AND THE SWEETNESS OF THE STRAWBERRIES, WHILE THE SWEET BALSAMIC GLAZE CONTRASTS WITH THE PEPPERY ROCKET. WHO COULD HAVE THOUGHT ALL THESE FLAVOURS COULD COME TOGETHER? TOSS IN SOME CORN AND YOU'VE CREATED A PICTURE PERFECT PINTXOS.

200g rump steak
salt and pepper to taste
hot mustard for spreading
1–2 Tbsp vegetable oil for grilling
½ cup corn kernels
butter for spreading
12 slices French baguette, lightly toasted
12 rocket leaves

6 strawberries, finely sliced
6 baby tomatoes, halved
2 balls buffalo mozzarella, torn into
  bite-size pieces
balsamic glaze
toothpicks or skewers (optional)

1. Generously season both sides of the meat with salt and pepper and spread on some hot mustard.
2. Heat a griddle pan and some oil until hot, then grill the meat for a few minutes, turn and continue to grill on the other side.
3. Once cooked to your liking (I like it medium rare), remove the meat from the pan and set it aside to rest for about 10 minutes.
4. While the meat is resting, dry-fry the corn in a pan until it starts to char. Remove and set aside.
5. To assemble, slice the steak thickly and butter the toasted baguette.
6. Place a rocket leaf on top of each slice of bread, add a slice or two of steak, about 2 slices of strawberry, half a baby tomato, followed by a piece of buffalo mozzarella and finally a scattering of charred corn. Finish each slice off with a drizzle of balsamic glaze. Hold everything together with a toothpick or skewer if necessary.

Beef & horseradish pintxos

Colourful beef pintxos

LITTLE LAMB CHOPS

INTRODUCE A LITTLE SUNSHINE INTO YOUR DAY WHATEVER THE WEATHER WITH THESE GLORIOUS LAMB CHOPS, SERVED WITH CAULIFLOWER PURÉE AND HARISSA ROASTED TOMATOES. HARISSA IS A TUNISIAN CHILLI PASTE MADE FROM RED PEPPERS, GARLIC, CORIANDER AND A TON OF OTHER FANTASTICALLY FRAGRANT FLAVOURS, ALL MIXED TOGETHER WITH OIL. HARISSA PROVIDES A SPICE-INDUCED METABOLIC BOOST, WHICH MEANS THAT YOU'LL BURN MORE CALORIES IMMEDIATELY FOLLOWING YOUR MEAL. THIS SPICY BLEND WILL QUICKLY BECOME YOUR NEW FAVOURITE CONDIMENT, TURNING LAMB FROM ORDINARY TO EXTRAORDINARY.

2 Tbsp olive oil
2 tsp finely chopped garlic
2 tsp honey
16 small lamb chops
salt and pepper to taste
2 Tbsp finely chopped mint leaves to garnish

CAULIFLOWER PURÉE
1 head cauliflower
2 Tbsp low fat yoghurt
salt and pepper to taste

HARISSA TOMATOES
32 small tomatoes, halved
salt and pepper to taste
2 tsp harissa paste
olive oil for drizzling

1. Preheat the oven to 180°C.
2. To make the cauliflower purée, break the cauliflower head into florets and boil in some salted water until softened. Drain the water, add the yoghurt and, using a stick blender, blend until puréed. Season with salt and pepper and set aside.
3. In a small bowl, combine the olive oil, garlic and honey.
4. Season the lamb chops generously on both sides with salt and pepper and spread the honey mixture over both sides.
5. On a heated griddle pan, grill the lamb chops until cooked to your liking, about 4 minutes per side. Once cooked, remove, keep warm and let rest while preparing the tomatoes.
6. To make the tomatoes, place the tomatoes on a greased baking sheet, season with salt and pepper and spread the harissa paste over them. Drizzle with some olive oil and bake for 5–10 minutes or until the tomatoes have softened but have still retained their shape. Remove and set aside.
7. To plate, add a dollop of cauliflower purée to each lamb chop, top with about 2–3 halved tomatoes and scatter over some chopped mint as garnish.

NESTED SPAGHETTI BOLOGNESE

SPAGHETTI BOLOGNESE IS A TIMELESS ITALIAN DISH THAT IS POPULAR ACROSS THE BOARD AND IS NOW REINVENTED IN THESE NIFTY LITTLE SPAGHETTI NESTS. BUT PASTA IS NOT HEALTHY, I HEAR YOU SAY? WELL, IT CAN BE BAD FOR YOU WHEN CONSUMED IN LARGE QUANTITIES IN CREAMY SAUCES, BUT WHEN EATEN IN MODERATE QUANTITIES IT CAN PROVIDE A HEALTHY CARB BASE FOR AN INFINITE VARIETY OF DISHES. NO MORE SLURPING AT THE DINNER TABLE WITH THESE HANDY BOLOGNESE BITES.

175g raw spaghetti
1 egg, beaten
1 cup grated Parmesan cheese
1 onion, finely chopped
250g lean beef mince
oil for frying
4 tsp Worcestershire sauce
1 x 400g tin chopped tomatoes

1 cup water
2 tsp tomato paste
1 tsp dried thyme
1 tsp dried sweet basil
1 chicken stock cube
salt and pepper to taste
½ cup grated Cheddar cheese
small fresh basil leaves for garnishing

1. Cook the spaghetti according to the packet instructions but remove the pasta just before it's cooked *al dente*. Drain and allow to cool slightly.
2. Add the beaten egg to the pasta and mix through thoroughly, then stir in the Parmesan cheese. Set aside and chill for 10 minutes.
3. Fry the onion and mince in a little oil until the mince is completely browned.
4. Stir in the Worcestershire sauce, tomatoes, water, tomato paste, thyme and basil.
5. Crumble in the stock cube and season with salt and pepper. Stir, then simmer for about 20 minutes.
6. Preheat the oven to 180°C.
7. In a greased muffin tin, line each hollow with the spaghetti, making an indentation in the middle.
8. Add about 1 tablespoon of mince into each 'nest' and drape additional spaghetti strands around the outside of the mince.
9. Place in the oven and bake for about 10 minutes.
10. Remove the tin from the oven, scatter over some Cheddar and place under the grill for about 5 minutes or until the cheese has melted and turned golden.
11. Remove the tin from the oven and allow to cool slightly. Using 2 spoons, carefully remove each nest and place on a serving plate. Don't attempt this too early as they might break when still hot. Garnish with fresh basil and serve.

DESSERT

Breakfast, lunch and dinner are all well and good, but they're very much about sustaining your body and giving it all the nutrients it needs. Dessert is where food really comes out to play. There are few sights more satisfying than a table decked out with a multitude of dazzling desserts. I love the way a table filled with fancy sweet treats can look like a treasure chest spilling over with jewels, each individual dish so colourful and vibrant.

I mean honestly, why would you have one dessert when you can have a little taste of everything? These dessert recipes are perfect for events where you are noshing on nibbles while chit-chatting with your family and friends. It's these types of occasion where having a table loaded up with mini desserts and serving a lavish assortment of puddings and pastries is a sure-fire way to put a smile on everybody's face.

Finish your event in style with decadent chocolate, marshmallow and fruit skewers, luscious lemon custard cups or petite pistachio cheese puffs. No matter which recipes you decide to make, these stunning yet simple desserts are sure to impress, and the petite portions are ideal for finishing off a filling meal.

BISCUIT & LEMON CUSTARD TEACUPS

THIS LUSCIOUS LEMON DESSERT IS SIMPLE TO MAKE, IS INCREDIBLY DELICIOUS AND IT'S BEEN A FIRM FAVOURITE IN MY FAMILY FOR YEARS. WITH MARIE BISCUITS THAT ARE DRENCHED IN A SMOOTH, CREAMY AND NOT TOO SOUR LEMON CURD, IT'S LOADED WITH VITAMIN C TO HELP KEEP THAT SCURVY AT BAY. DELICATELY LAYERED INTO A TEACUP, IT'S A CUTE AND CREATIVE TEATIME (OR ANYTIME) PUDDING WITH A ZESTY, LEMONY FLAVOUR THAT EVERYONE WILL LOVE.

1 cup lemon juice
⅓ cup lemon zest
1 x 385g tin condensed milk
¾ x 100g packet Marie biscuits
1¼ cups custard, ready made

1. In a bowl, combine the lemon juice and zest with the condensed milk. Beat the mixture until the stickiness disappears.
2. Place one Marie biscuit into the base of a teacup. Alternatively, break the biscuit into pieces to fit your teacup.
3. Add about 2 tablespoons of custard on top of the biscuit, followed by another biscuit.
4. Add about 2 tablespoons of the condensed milk mixture on top of the biscuit.
5. Crumble half a biscuit on top and serve.

YOGHURT & CARAMEL BITES

THIS RECIPE LETS YOU TURN REGULAR YOGHURT INTO FANTASTIC FROZEN BITE-SIZE TREATS. GREEK YOGHURT IS ONE OF MY FAVOURITE INGREDIENTS BECAUSE IT IS SO RICH IN PROBIOTICS, WHICH ARE EXCELLENT FOR GOOD GUT HEALTH. ALL YOU NEED IS YOGHURT, FRUIT, CARAMEL AND A FREEZER AND YOU CAN CREATE A SNACK THAT WILL SATISFY ANY SWEET TOOTH. FAIR WARNING: ONCE YOU START ON THESE, YOU'LL FIND IT VERY DIFFICULT TO STOP.

½ x 200g packet plain digestive biscuits
3 Tbsp butter
½ cup Greek yoghurt
½ cup blueberries, halved
2 Tbsp sugar-free strawberry jam
⅓ cup caramel

1. Place the biscuits into a sealable bag and, using a rolling pin, break the biscuits into crumbs.
2. Melt the butter and combine with the crumbs.
3. Place a paper cupcake holder into each muffin cup, add a spoonful of biscuit mixture and press down to form a crust on the base.
4. In a bowl, combine the yoghurt and blueberries.
5. Gently swirl the jam into the yoghurt mixture, creating a marbled effect. Don't overmix or you risk losing the marble effect.
6. Heat the caramel to make it runnier and place a spoonful on top of the biscuit crust.
7. Add a tablespoon or two of yoghurt mixture on top of the caramel and place in the freezer to set.
8. When ready to serve, remove from the freezer and serve immediately.

FRUIT PIZZA

THERE'S NOTHING LIKE A GOOD SLICE OF REFRESHING, THIRST-QUENCHING FRUIT ON A HOT SUMMER'S DAY, BUT IT'S EVEN BETTER WHEN SERVED AS A MOUTHWATERING PIZZA DESSERT. MOVE OVER, MAIN COURSE – PIZZA ISN'T JUST FOR LUNCHTIME ANY MORE. THIS FRUIT PIZZA RECIPE OFFERS A SWEET, HEALTHY TREAT THAT'S LIGHT, REFRESHING AND NUTRITIOUS. THIS IS THE PERFECT DESSERT FOR THE WHOLE FAMILY AND WILL HAVE EVERYONE GRABBING SLICES ALMOST AS FAST AS YOU CAN SERVE THEM.

1–2 cups seasonal fruit, sliced or chopped
2½ Tbsp custard powder
2 Tbsp sugar
1¼ cup milk
2 flour tortillas
honey for drizzling
finely grated lime zest for decorating

1. Blend the custard powder and sugar with a splash of milk to form a smooth paste.
2. Heat the balance of the milk until almost boiling and stir in the custard paste.
3. Bring the custard mixture to a boil, stirring until the mixture has thickened.
4. Remove from the heat and allow to cool.
5. In a pan, toast both sides of each tortilla until browned and crisp.
6. Spoon half the custard onto one tortilla and place the other tortilla on top.
7. Spoon over the balance of the custard and arrange the fruit on top.
8. Drizzle over the honey and scatter over the grated lime zest.

PISTACHIO FIG CHEESE PUFFS

THESE BEAUTIFULLY BALANCED MORSELS COMBINE FLAKY, BUTTERY PASTRY WITH SWEET BUT SUBTLE FIGS. I LOVE SERVING THESE AS A STARTER OR TO ROUND OFF A DINNER WITH FRIENDS AND FAMILY. THE CLASSIC CHEESE PUFF RECIPE GETS A DELICIOUS UPDATE WITH THE ADDITION OF PISTACHIOS AND FIG. PISTACHIOS ARE AN EXCELLENT NUT TO USE SINCE THEY'RE HIGH IN NUTRIENTS BUT LOW IN CALORIES, WHICH MEANS YOU CAN GET AWAY WITH ONE OR TWO MORE PUFFS. THEY'RE SIMPLE YET ELEGANT AND ARE GUARANTEED TO DISAPPEAR AS QUICKLY AS THEY ARE SERVED.

---

7 Tbsp cream cheese

5 Tbsp crumbled blue cheese

2 Tbsp shelled pistachio nuts plus extra for garnishing

1 tsp dried thyme

1 x 400g packet ready rolled puff pastry

1 egg yolk, lightly beaten

4–5 preserved figs

2 Tbsp fig preserve juice

1. Preheat the oven to 180°C.
2. Combine the cream and blue cheeses.
3. Grind together the pistachio nuts and thyme.
4. Using a 3cm cookie cutter, cut out circles from the ready rolled puff pastry.
5. Brush the circles with the egg yolk and generously scatter over the ground pistachio mixture, pressing down to ensure that the crumbs don't fall off.
6. Place on a greased baking sheet and bake in the oven for about 10 minutes or until the pastry is cooked and golden brown.
7. While the pastry is in the oven, cut the figs into bite-size pieces.
8. Remove the cooked puffs from the oven and, as soon as they are cool enough to handle, cut them in half horizontally.
9. Spread some cheese mixture onto the bottom half of each puff, add a piece of fig, drizzle over a touch of the fig juice and replace the top piece of pastry. Sprinkle with extra grated pistachio nuts.

MINI BAKLAVA CHEESECAKES

THESE DELECTABLE LITTLE DESSERTS ARE A FIRM FAVOURITE AMONG THOSE WITH A SWEET TOOTH. TWO BELOVED CULTURAL CUISINES MEET IN THE MOST DELICIOUS WAY POSSIBLE. WITH ALL THE FLAVOURS OF CINNAMON, THE HONEY (A SNEAKY WAY OF GETTING ANTIOXIDANTS INTO YOUR DESSERT) AND A VARIETY OF NUTS, IT'S A PLAYFUL WAY TO MIX TWO DESSERTS INTO ONE. THEY NOT ONLY TASTE INCREDIBLE BUT LOOK IMPRESSIVE TOO, SO YOU CAN WHIP THESE UP WHEN YOU WANT TO PUT OUT A DESSERT SPREAD THAT WILL DAZZLE YOUR GUESTS.

2 sheets phyllo pastry
melted butter
honey for drizzling
lemon juice for serving

NUT FILLING
16 pistachios
16 almonds
16 hazelnuts or walnuts
¾ tsp ground cinnamon
1½ Tbsp sugar

CHEESE FILLING
1 x 250g tub cream cheese
1 tsp custard powder
2 Tbsp sugar
1 egg
2 Tbsp milk
2 Tbsp Greek yoghurt

1. Preheat the oven to 170°C.
2. To make the phyllo tarts, cut out about 30 squares measuring 7cm from the phyllo pastry.
3. Dab a touch of melted butter in the middle of half of the squares, then add another square at right angles to each square and brush completely with melted butter.
4. In a greased muffin tin, carefully place the phyllo squares into each muffin hole.
5. To make the nut filling, chop all the nuts and combine with the cinnamon and sugar.
6. To make the cheese filling, blend all the ingredients together.
7. Place a teaspoon of the nut mixture into the base of each phyllo cup. There should be nuts left over for sprinkling over the cooked tartlets.
8. Pour about 1¼ tablespoons of the cheese filling over the nuts, just filling each tartlet.
9. Bake the tartlets in the oven for about 10 minutes. Be careful not to burn the phyllo.
10. Once the phyllo is golden and the cheese filling is only just wobbly, switch off the oven, leave the oven door ajar and allow the muffin tin to cool.
11. Remove and, when ready to serve, drizzle the tops with honey, add splashes of lemon juice and sprinkle over the remaining nuts.

DECONSTRUCTED ROOIBOS PANNA COTTA

TURN TEATIME INTO DESSERT TIME WITH THIS CLEVER TAKE ON A GOOD OLD CUP OF ROOIBOS TEA. ROOIBOS IS ONE OF THE PROUD JEWELS IN SOUTH AFRICA'S CULINARY CROWN AND ITS ONE OF A KIND FLAVOUR WORKS PERFECTLY IN THIS DECONSTRUCTED DESSERT. ROOIBOS TEA ALSO HAS NO CAFFEINE, SO YOU WON'T STAY UP ALL NIGHT AFTER YOUR MAGNIFICENT MEAL. THE TEA ADDS A WONDERFUL FLAVOUR TO THE CREAMY PANNA COTTA, AND LEMON AND HONEY CUT THE RICHNESS PERFECTLY. TRY THIS RECIPE THE NEXT TIME YOU ENTERTAIN AND SERVE YOUR GUESTS A SENSATIONAL PANNA COTTA CUPPA.

2 Tbsp powdered unflavoured gelatin
4 Tbsp cold water
6 cups whipping cream
3 cups milk
¼ cup honey
2 rooibos teabags

SYRUP
¼ cup honey
¼ cup lemon juice

3 Tbsp lemon zest for decorating
fresh mint leaves for decorating

1. In a small bowl, sprinkle the gelatin over the cold water and let it sponge for about 5 minutes.
2. Heat the cream, milk, honey and teabags in a pot on a medium heat until small bubbles form around the sides.
3. Remove from the heat and let the tea steep for about 3 minutes.
4. Remove the teabags from the cream mixture, then whisk in the gelatin until completely dissolved.
5. Divide the mixture among teacups, cover with clingfilm, making sure the plastic touches the mixture, and chill in the fridge until set.
6. When ready to serve, combine the honey and lemon and drizzle over the panna cotta.
7. Scatter over the lemon zest and decorate each panna cotta with mint leaves.

Mini baklava cheesecakes

Deconstructed
rooibos panna cotta

CHURRO CHIPS WITH CHOCOLATE SAUCE

YOU CAN NEVER HAVE TOO MANY QUICK AND EASY DESSERT RECIPES, AND THESE CHURRO CHIPS WITH A CHOCOLATE DIPPING SAUCE FIT THE BILL EXACTLY. THE CHIPS ARE CRISP AND BUTTERY AND COVERED WITH CINNAMON SUGAR. THE ADDITION OF THE RICH CHOCOLATE DIPPING SAUCE BRINGS THIS DESSERT OVER THE TOP. THEY SAY THAT THE SIMPLE THINGS IN LIFE ARE OFTEN THE BEST, AND THAT CERTAINLY COULDN'T BE MORE TRUE WHEN IT COMES TO CHURRO CHIPS.

1⅓ cups brown sugar
2 tsp ground cinnamon
16 flour tortillas
250g butter, melted

CHOCOLATE DIPPING SAUCE
½ cup sugar
4 tsp cornflour
4 tsp unsweetened cocoa powder
a pinch of salt
2 cups low-fat milk
2 tsp vanilla essence
160g dark chocolate, chopped

1. Preheat the oven to 180°C.
2. In a bowl, combine the sugar and cinnamon.
3. Using a pastry brush, coat both sides of each tortilla with melted butter and sprinkle each side with cinnamon sugar.
4. Make 2 stacks of tortillas comprising 8 tortillas each and cut each into 8 triangles.
5. Place the 16 stacked tortilla triangles on a large greased baking sheet and bake for 15–18 minutes, until they are browned and crisp. Allow to cool completely before removing them from the baking sheet.
6. To make the dipping sauce, combine the sugar, cornflour, cocoa powder and salt in a pot. Gradually stir in the milk until the mixture is smooth.
7. Heat the mixture over a medium heat, stirring constantly until it comes to the boil. Then lower the heat and simmer gently, stirring continuously for 3–4 minutes.
8. Stir in the vanilla essence and chopped dark chocolate until the chocolate melts and the ingredients are thoroughly combined. Serve with the churro chips.

LIQUORICE BISCUITS WITH STRAWBERRY & MASCARPONE

WHILE STRAWBERRIES MAY BE MADE UP OF SIMPLE SUGARS, THEIR FLAVOUR IS ANYTHING BUT SIMPLE. WITH A LOW GI AND AN ABUNDANCE OF VITAMINS, STRAWBERRIES ARE THE HEALTHIEST WEAPON IN YOUR DESSERT ARSENAL. THEY HAVE A UNIQUE FRUITY FLAVOUR, AND THIS RECIPE BLENDS THAT TOGETHER WITH THE SWEET, SPICY TASTE OF FENNEL TO CREATE A PERFECT PAIRING. CRISP, CRUNCHY BISCUITS ARE COMPLEMENTED BY CREAMY NOTES OF THE MASCARPONE AND THE ZESTY TONES OF THE STRAWBERRY. IT'S A MOUTHWATERING MATCH MADE IN HEAVEN THAT WILL HAVE EVERYONE ON THE BLOCK ASKING FOR A SECOND HELPING.

300g cake wheat flour
1¼ tsp baking powder
1 tsp salt
3 Tbsp fennel seeds, finely ground
⅓ cup sugar
¼ cup vegetable oil

1 egg, lightly beaten
½ cup warm water
mascarpone cheese for spreading
15–20 sliced strawberries for decorating
1 long piece plain black liquorice, finely
    chopped, for decorating

1. Preheat the oven to 180°C.
2. In a bowl, combine the flour, baking powder, salt and fennel seeds.
3. In a large bowl, combine the sugar, oil and egg and beat until blended and pale yellow.
4. Fold in the flour mixture and add the water a little bit at a time until the mixture forms a soft dough.
5. Transfer the dough to a lightly floured work surface and knead for 2 or 3 minutes, then divide into 3 equal portions as it's easier to work with smaller portions.
6. Lightly flour the work surface and roll out 1 portion of the dough to create a 20cm square.
7. Using a 4–5cm cookie cutter, cut circles out of the dough.
8. Repeat with the 2 remaining portions of dough.
9. Place the dough circles onto a greased baking sheet and bake for 15–20 minutes.
10. Cool the biscuits on a rack, and when ready to serve, spread a teaspoon or two of mascarpone cheese on each biscuit, followed by some sliced strawberries and a scattering of liquorice.

SWEET DELIGHTS

WHEN YOU PUT FOOD ON A STICK, PEOPLE JUST CAN'T SEEM TO RESIST. SO, WHEN YOU TURN THAT INTO A DESSERT, YOU HAVE A SURE-FIRE SENSATION ON YOUR HANDS. POPULAR WITH KIDS AND ADULTS ALIKE, THESE COLOURFUL DESSERT SKEWERS CAN BE PREPARED IN MINUTES. THESE ARE SO IRRESISTIBLY DELICIOUS AND PRETTY, YOUR GUESTS WILL WANT TO SKIP DINNER AND HEAD STRAIGHT FOR DESSERT. THEIR ONLY PROBLEM WILL BE TO DECIDE WHICH SKEWERS TO TAKE FIRST, SO BE PREPARED TO MAKE ENOUGH OF BOTH.

STRAWBERRY DELIGHTS
8–12 strawberries
6–8 marshmallows
12–16 Cadbury Whispers

toothpicks
balsamic glaze for drizzling

BANANA DELIGHTS
2 bananas
4 Tbsp sugar
2 Tbsp ground cinnamon
4 Tbsp honey
2 pancakes, ready-made

1. To make the strawberry delights, cut the strawberries in half if they are large. Cut the marshmallows in half.
2. To assemble, spear half a marshmallow, followed by a strawberry and then carefully add a Whisper. Don't push the toothpick all the way through the Whisper as it might break.
3. To make the banana delights, cut the bananas into rounds. Combine the sugar and cinnamon.
4. Spread the honey over the pancakes and scatter over the cinnamon sugar, then cut into strips. Roll up each strip like a Swiss roll.
5. To assemble, thread a pancake roll onto each toothpick, followed by a slice of banana, then another roll of pancake and finally another slice of banana.
6. Just before serving, drizzle some balsamic glaze over both desserts.

Liquorice biscuits with strawberry & mascarpone

Strawberry delights

Banana delights

TIPSY TRUFFLES

SINFULLY DELICIOUS, THESE BOOZY BITES WILL QUICKLY BECOME ONE OF YOUR GO-TO DESSERT RECIPES. THIS DECADENT PARTNERSHIP OF SPIRITS AND CHOCOLATE IS RICH, SWEET AND SIMPLY DIVINE. THE BEST PART? THEY SOUND SO MUCH FANCIER THAN THEY ARE TO MAKE. SPIKED WITH LIQUEUR, SIMPLE AND EASY TO MAKE, YOU CAN FINISH OFF ANY MEAL IN STYLE WITH THIS TIPSY TRIO OF TROUBLE. THEY ARE LUXURIOUS, INTOXICATING, AND OH, SO MORE-ISH. THERE ARE ENDLESS POSSIBILITIES, BUT HERE ARE THREE VARIETIES, ALL WITH THE SAME METHOD OF PREPARATION.

COFFEE LIQUEUR
200g 70% dark chocolate
½ cup cream
8 Tbsp coffee liqueur
ground espresso for coating

PEACH SCHNAPPS
200g white milk chocolate
¼ cup cream
6 Tbsp peach schnapps
desiccated coconut for coating

AMARULA LIQUEUR
200g 70% dark chocolate
½ cup cream
8 Tbsp Amarula cream
cocoa powder for coating

1. Melt the chocolate in a double boiler or in a microwave. Don't allow the chocolate to boil.
2. In a separate container, heat the cream, but don't let it boil.
3. Pour the cream and liqueur into the melted chocolate and stir until well combined.
4. Place the chocolate mixture in the fridge and allow it to harden until almost set, about 2 hours.
5. For each truffle, use your hands to roll about a tablespoon of chocolate mixture into a ball, then place on a silicone mat or a flat plate covered with baking paper.
6. Roll the balls in the appropriate coatings and place back on the baking paper and back in the fridge to set.

FRUIT SOUP

WHO SAYS YOU CAN'T HAVE SOUP FOR DESSERT? SERVE YOUR GUESTS A TASTE OF THE TROPICS WITH THIS CHILLED, SWEET SIPPER. INSPIRED BY BEACH TRIPS, PALM TREES AND ENDLESS SUNSETS, THIS MANGO AND GRANADILLA-FLAVOURED SOUP TASTES LIKE AN ISLAND HOLIDAY FEELS – BALMY, EXTRAVAGANT AND DREAMY. EASY, PEASY, TROPICAL BREEZY. THIS RECIPE IS A MAXIMUM VITAMIN BOOSTER, CHOCK FULL OF VITAMINS A, B AND C AS WELL AS ZINC. IT MAY SEEM UNUSUAL BUT AFTER ONE EXPERIENCE WITH FRUIT SOUP, YOU'LL BE A CONVERT FOR LIFE.

2 mangoes, peeled and chopped
4 granadillas, pulp only
1 cup sparkling water
vanilla ice cream for serving
desiccated and/or flaked coconut for decorating

1. In a blender, blitz the mango and granadilla into a pulp.
2. Stir in the sparkling water.
3. Chill well until ready to serve.
4. Pour into pretty glasses, add a dollop of ice cream and a generous sprinkle of coconut.

CHOCOLATE MINT & APPLE PARCELS

THESE CHOCOLATE MINT AND APPLE PARCELS ARE BEST DESCRIBED IN THREE WORDS – TO, DIE, FOR. THESE FABULOUS FINGER FOODS HAVE AN INDULGENT LAYER OF CHOCOLATE AND A FRESH, FRUITY APPLE AND MINT CENTRE. WHILE THEY ARE EVERY BIT AS DELICIOUS AS APPLE PIE, THE ADDITION OF CHOCOLATE AND MINT IS A TOTAL GAME-CHANGER. MINT IS WELL KNOWN FOR AIDING DIGESTION, SO YOU CAN SERVE THESE PARCELS EVEN WHEN THERE'S ONLY ROOM FOR ONE MORE BITE. THE MIXTURE OF TEXTURES AND FLAVOURS TURNS SOMETHING TRADITIONAL INTO EVERYTHING YOU COULD EVER WANT IN ONE DESSERT.

3–4 cups diced red apples, unpeeled
¼ cup water
¼ cup chopped fresh mint
1 Tbsp white sugar
2 x 400g packets ready rolled puff pastry
⅔ cup chocolate spread (such as Nutella)
2 egg yolks, beaten
2 tsp brown sugar

1. Preheat the oven to 180°C.
2. Place the diced apples, water, 2 tablespoons of chopped mint and the sugar in a pot and cook the apples until they have just softened, 5–10 minutes. Remove, drain and allow to cool.
3. Cut each roll of pastry into 9 squares.
4. Spread 1 teaspoon of chocolate spread onto each square.
5. Scatter over some chopped mint and arrange some apple pieces on top.
6. Take opposite corners of each pastry square and bring them together, then do the same with the other corners. Squeeze the edges together, forming a closed parcel.
7. Brush each square with egg yolk and sprinkle over some brown sugar.
8. Place on a greased baking sheet and bake in the oven for about 15 minutes or until the pastry is cooked and golden.
9. Remove from the oven and allow to cool.

RECIPE INDEX

goat's milk cheese 23

Fish and seafood

Calamari, chorizo & patatas bravas 74

Hake goujons with a quartet of sauces 82

Oysters on leeks 91

Pepper-crusted tuna with wasabi mayo 70

Prawn & mushroom pintxos 92

Red pepper pesto & corn salsa mussels 88

Salmon & baby marrow skewers 78

Salmon on potato slices with dill cream 84

Smoked mussel fish cakes with Thai green curry dressing 73

Smoked salmon, scrambled egg & saffron cucumber bites 14

Smoked snoek pâté on seed loaf 75

Tuna-stuffed pepper pintxos 81

Yellowtail ceviche 85

Flavoured cheese straws 47

French toast bites with strawberry & honey sauce 19

Fruits, berries and nuts

Avocado toast with prosciutto, pear & brie 27

Banana delights 165

Bobotie cups 128

Cheesy herb muffins with peppadew cream 66

Chia seed powerhouse 15

Chocolate mint & apple parcels 172

Colourful beef pintxos 141

Cubed pork belly on apple slices 136

Curried chicken mini pitas with mango mayo 106

French toast bites with strawberry & honey sauce 19

Fruit pizza 155

Fruit soup 171

Granadilla chicken on potato slices 119

Liquorice biscuits with strawberry & mascarpone 165

Mini baklava cheesecakes 158

Mini rice cakes with hummus & pickled carrot 53

Pistachio fig cheese puffs 156

Ricotta-stuffed dates wrapped in bacon 24

Spicy pork mini tacos 122

Strawberry delights 165

Sweet chilli chicken balls on nachos 115

Yellowtail ceviche 85

Yoghurt & caramel bites 152

Fruit pizza 155

Fruit soup 171

Gazpacho shooters 41

Gourmet 'hot dog' pintxos 139

Granadilla chicken on potato slices 119

Green tea chicken pintxos 112

Hake goujons with a quartet of sauces 82

Honey

Avocado toast with prosciutto, pear & brie 27

Butternut & gnocchi bites 40

Carrot & pea triangles 46

Chia seed powerhouse 15

Cubed pork belly on apple slices 136

Deconstructed rooibos panna cotta 159

French toast bites with strawberry & honey sauce 19

Little lamb chops 145

Mini baklava cheesecakes 158

Pepper-crusted tuna with wasabi mayo 70

Prawn & mushroom pintxos 92

lamb chops, Little 145

lamb tapas, Moroccan 125

Leek filling 58

Liquorice biscuits with strawberry & mascarpone 165

Little lamb chops 145

marinade for Mini skewered chicken with a peanut coconut sauce 105

marinade, Curry 106

Mediterranean chicken pintxos 108

Mini baklava cheesecakes 158

Mini naan bread baskets 50

Mini rice cakes with hummus & pickled carrot 53

Mini skewered chicken with a peanut coconut sauce 105

Moroccan lamb tapas 125

Moroccan spice 125

muffins, Cheese & herb 66

Mushrooms

Arancini with truffle dip 96

Beef lollipop pies 126

Breakfast slices 30

Chicken blue cheese bites 116

Mediterranean chicken pintxos 108

Mushroom filling 58

Prawn & mushroom pintxos 92

Mustard

Beef & horseradish pintxos 140

Beetroot & halloumi skewers 39

Caesar-style eggs 31

Cheese & mustard sauce 109

Colourful beef pintxos 141

Dipped baked pretzels 36

Gourmet 'hot dog' pintxos 139

Smoked mussel fish cakes with Thai green curry dressing 73

Wholegrain mustard sauce 108

Nested spaghetti Bolognese 146

nori, Crisp 55

Olives

Cucumber ribbons with feta & olive spread 61

Peppadew pintxos 65

ostrich slices, Raspberry chutney 132

Oysters on leeks 91

Pastry

Beef lollipop pies 126

Caramelised onion & goat's milk cheese tartlets 45

Carrot & pea triangles 46

Chocolate mint & apple parcels 172

Chunky phyllo cigars with anchovy cream cheese filling 13

Flavoured cheese straws 47

Mini baklava cheesecakes 158

Pistachio fig cheese puffs 156

Pea purée 125

Peppadew pintxos 65

Pepper-crusted tuna with wasabi mayo 70

Pickled asparagus 108

Pickled carrots 53

Pintxos

Beef & horseradish pintxos 140

Colourful beef pintxos 141

Gourmet 'hot dog' pintxos 139

Green tea chicken pintxos 112

Mediterranean chicken pintxos 108

Peppadew pintxos 65

Prawn & mushroom pintxos 92

Salami, egg & chips pintxos 10

Tuna-stuffed pepper pintxos 81

Pistachio fig cheese puffs 156

Pita fries with za'atar & feta 54

pitas, Curried chicken mini, with mango mayo 106

Pork

Artichoke & Parma ham skewers 135

Avocado toast with prosciutto, pear & brie 27

Beef lollipop pies 126

Breakfast slices 30

Caesar-style eggs 31

Cubed pork belly on apple slices 136

Deconstructed chicken cordon bleu 109

Eggs *en cocotte* with tomato & goat's milk cheese 23

Gourmet 'hot dog' pintxos 139

Potato 'toasts' with egg, sumac & pea spread 20

Ricotta-stuffed dates wrapped in bacon 24

Salami, egg & chips pintxos 10

Spicy pork mini tacos 122

Potato 'toasts' with egg, sumac & pea spread 20

Potato & onion tortilla 28

Prawn & mushroom pintxos 92

pretzels, Dipped baked 36

Raita 129

Raspberry chutney ostrich slices 132

Red pepper pesto & corn salsa mussels 88

Rice cups 128